WHITE-MAN-RUNS-HIM

CROW SCOUT WITH CUSTER

BY

DENNIS W. HARCEY

AND

BRIAN R. CROONE

WITH

JOE MEDICINE CROW

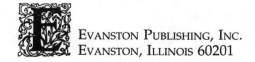
EVANSTON PUBLISHING, INC.
EVANSTON, ILLINOIS 60201

Evanston Publishing, Inc.
1520 Sherman Avenue, Annex C
EVANSTON, IL 60201

Library of Congress Preassigned Catalog Card Number: 93-070274

Printed in the USA
All Rights Reserved

10 9 8 7 6 5 4 3

ISBN: 1-879260-36-0

Cover illustration by Ramona Medicine Crow

ABOUT THE AUTHORS

Dennis Harcey attended the University of Wisconsin Eau Claire and received a B.S. degree in 1961. He received his M.S. Degree from the University of Wisconsin, Eau Claire, with major concentration in history and anthropology in 1969. His thesis concentrated on the Winnebago Culture of Wisconsin.

Harcey has received numerous scholarships and fellowships from a variety of institutions including the University of Minnesota; the University of Wisconsin; the University of Georgia; Grove City College, Pennsylvania; Hillsdale College, Michigan; Carleton College; Macalester College, Minnesota; Irvington on the Hudson, N.Y.; and the Buffalo Bill Historical Society, Cody, Wyoming. In his 31 years of teaching experience, he has taught Social Problems, United States History, and World History.

Harcey along with Brian Croone founded an annual lecture series entitled "Big Woods/Big Plains" in 1987. The highly successful three-day program brings in experts from Minnesota and around the nation to speak on Native American history and/or culture. The program continues to grow in numbers and popularity and is unique in that it is the only annual lecture series of its kind in the country.

Brian Croone graduated from the University of Minnesota, Duluth in 1979 with a B. S. in Education, concentrating in history. In 1981, he received a degree in Special Education from Bemidji State College. Croone began his teaching career at Stillwater Senior High, Stillwater, Minnesota, in 1979, where he has taught senior high students. He specializes in both United States and World History.

Croone has received a number of scholarships and fellowships which have provided him with the opportunity to attend Stanford University; the D'Arcy McNickle Center; Newberry Library, Chicago; East Central University, Ada, Oklahoma; and the Buffalo Bill Historic Center, Cody, Wyoming.

DEDICATION

We would like to dedicate this work to Joe Medicine Crow, currently Tribal Anthropologist, Archaeologist, and Historian of the Crow Nation; a man who feels responsibility for and continues to work daily on behalf of his people and their cultural and historical survival. Joe is a man of great foresight and intelligence, whose interest and record keeping began when just a child, pursuing his elders for any piece of knowledge he could glean. He was the first Crow male to achieve a college diploma and is only a thesis away from his Ph.D.

Medicine Crow served his country with distinction in World War II, and was greatly honored by his elders who conferred upon him the title of War Chief for the honors he achieved during the conflict. In fact, he is the last legitimate War Chief of the Crow people.

He is also a published author, having written several books and numerous articles and pamphlets. He wrote and directed a recreation of the Battle of the Little Big Horn that played near the site of the original conflict, and toured the Battlefield with many of the old scouts and warriors who fought with and against Custer. He listened to their stories, and he listened well. His memory is accurate beyond question. Authors seek him out on almost all questions involving the Crow, and in the tradition of his grandfathers, Medicine Crow and White- Man-Run-Him, he has answered the call to serve others.

Joe continues to teach at the Little Big Horn College and his collections of speeches and documents are a most valuable tool for the historian or researcher. Medicine Crow is in demand as a lecturer and both advises and sits on a number of regional and national committees.

Medicine Crow will never retire. His search for truth and justice, his trust and faith in others, and his appreciation for all that is good, combined with his sense of humor, have already won for him a place in the sacred sanctuary of the Great Beyond. We thank Joe Medicine Crow for his efforts on behalf of this book, for without his help it would not have been written.

A SPECIAL NOTE OF THANKS

We would especially like to thank Joe Medicine Crow for his patience and endurance during the extensive interview process. His knowledge, wisdom, and understanding contributed greatly in facilitating this work. We would also like to thank Winona Plenty Hoops for sharing her understanding of White-Man-Runs-Him with us. Credit should also be given to the descendants of White-Man-Runs-Him whose input both direct and indirect was invaluable.

Special acknowledgment should be given to the Smithsonian Institute, the Historical Societies of Minnesota, Montana, North Dakota, Pennsylvania, Wyoming, and the American Baptist Historical Society, the Billings Public Library, the Little Big Horn College Library, the Little Big Horn Battlefield Library, Mankato State University Library, the Newberry Library, the Stillwater Public Library, and the University of Minnesota Library, for their assistance in opening their records, loaning materials when possible, and aiding the process of research.

We would also like to thank Chester Medicine Crow for his drawing of one of White-Man-Runs-Him's tepees, and Ramona Medicine Crow for painting the picture used on the cover. Accolades are also in order for Merwyn Brown of Stillwater, Minnesota, for the map and sketch work used throughout the text.

Recognition and praise is in order for Gary Zabel, English Department Chairman, and Laurie Hansen, Journalism and Publications Instructor, Stillwater Senior High, Stillwater, Minnesota for editing the manuscript. To Beverly Walmar of Lake Elmo, Minnesota, for the many hours spent in typing and retyping the manuscript goes our most sincere gratitude.

INTRODUCTION

In 1987, while attending a class on Native American History and Culture at the Buffalo Bill Historic Center, Cody, Wyoming we became interested in Indian history and culture. During the two week seminar, which included lectures, discussions, and travel experience to the historic sites of Montana, it occurred to us that we could do our part to enhance Native American concerns and their rich heritage by developing an annual symposium in Stillwater, Minnesota.

When we returned to Stillwater, we did just that by setting up a program called Big Woods/Big Plains. Dr. Herman Viola, National Anthropological Archives, our instructor at Cody, encouraged our efforts. He, along with Joe Medicine Crow, Crow Tribal Historian, and George Horse Capture, then Curator at the Buffalo Bill Historic Center's Indian Museum, were the major and featured speakers at our first seminar. The program was a success beyond our expectations.

While we developed a close friendship with Viola, Horse Capture, and Medicine Crow over the years, we became especially close to Medicine Crow whom we have visited in Montana every year since. After consultation with Medicine Crow, and coming to understand his busy schedule and his desire to have a book written on White-Man-Runs-Him, we agreed to be the instrument that would attempt to produce such a book with his help.

Viola had told us that he considers Medicine Crow to be a "National Treasure." After spending a number of summers with this talented and knowledgeable gentleman, we agreed with Viola's assessment of Medicine Crow. With him we toured the Crow Reservation, saw the ancient sites, traveled the route taken by White-Man-Runs-Him and Custer to the Little Big Horn, and gained an appreciation for the ways of a proud and historic people.

While on the Crow reservation, we came to better understand the life and the man called White-Man-Runs-Him. He grew up in a traditional Crow setting, adopting the values and goals of a warrior society. As a young man White-Man-Runs-Him accomplished many of his personal and tribal goals, but he was frustrated and prevented from gaining full chieftainship primarily due to the rapid advance of the whites into Crow land and the ensuing cultural changes. He enlisted in the military in part to protect tribal lands from the Sioux and Cheyenne, and in part to gain honors in war. White-Man-Runs-Him learned quickly that he had to adapt to the new ways in order to maintain Crow lands and the survival of his people.

White-Man-Runs-Him realized the whites were sometimes hypocritical in their relations with the Crow, and yet he noted the good and the positive benefits in those he came to trust. Until his death, he would remain loyal to the American flag under which he served. Even though he did not always agree with Custer or his decisions, he always viewed Custer with great respect.

White-Man-Runs-Him became a student of history, attempting throughout his life to answer the unanswered questions concerning the Battle of the Little Big Horn. He was much sought after by historians for his knowledge, and he tried to meet the demands on his time.

He became involved in politics, representing his tribe in Washington as a delegate on a number of occasions. He talked with Presidents, and he defended what he believed was right. His handsome features and good natured personality made him one of the most photographed Indians of his time. His features were so exceptional that he was selected to be the model for the Wanamaker Memorial to the American Indian, to be built in the New York Harbor at a height greater than the Statue of Liberty.

He was always in demand at parades, celebrations, and dedications. Dignitaries referred to him as the "popular old scout," and yet he had to struggle to gain a pension from the government whose army he served. In the end, he would convert to the Baptist faith, and when he died in 1929, he was mourned from all corners of the nation. The legacy of White-Man-Runs-Him is alive today and still flourishes in the land of the Crow.

In attempting to reconstruct the life of White-Man-Runs-Him, we were limited only by the incomplete and sometimes inaccurate records that perhaps had been put together by officials with little time, little interest or both. There is little doubt that until Crow children had received an education, and returned with an understanding of English, much of what was translated from the Crow was misunderstood and inaccurate. In some cases we found records missing, or not available. And then too, there are many gaps in the life of White-Man-Runs-Him, because during those times records and data that we take for granted were not kept.

Medicine Crow and the elders we interviewed taught us that oral tradition is still well in place among the Crow, and we might add, very accurate. We are grateful for the opportunity to become acquainted with those people of the Crow who are now with the generation that will be the last to have known White-Man-Runs-Him.

CONTENTS

I. THE SEARCH FOR THE RIGHT PLACE

Many years ago in the Middle East, Moses led the nation of Israel across the Red Sea into the Sinai. After wandering for 40 years in the desert, they were finally delivered to the promised land, a land flowing with milk and honey. In a like manner, the ancestors of the modern Crow Nation roamed for hundreds of years in the wilderness until they, too, were directed by the Creator to the right place — the promised land of the Crow.

Ethnologists have long considered the Crow as part of the Siouan linguistic stock. If the classifications are correct, then the ancestors of the modern Crow were part of the great migration of Siouan peoples that began to move from a homeland on the Atlantic coast sometime before the coming of Columbus.

While in the East, the Siouan people occupied an area of approximately 70,000 square miles along the eastern foothills of the Southern Alleghenies, including all of central Virginia, two-thirds of North Carolina, and all of the northeastern portion of South Carolina. The location of these woodland people put them in a position of being in constant conflict with Iroquoian, Algonquin, and Muskhogean tribes. The pressures of battle no doubt contributed to or caused the great movement toward the West. The ancestors of the modern Crow were part of this migration which took place over centuries. It seems reasonable to assume that as the migration began it was little different from other prehistoric migrations, that there was no specific objective in mind, and that the journey was interrupted from time to time as the tribe found new agricultural and hunting areas.

The Crow have no oral history that would account for the movement from the eastern seaboard. Their oral history of Crow migration begins when the tribe lived "south of Lake Superior and east of Lake Michigan."

There is much evidence that indicates that the Crow were curious and even speculated about their past, including the time before their origin story begins. Pretty Shield, wife of Goes Ahead, a scout with Custer, often wondered, as did many other Crow, about whether the Crow had at one time lived in the South or had been in contact with a people who did. Her interest had been stimulated by the use of the word *Bilakse* or "Father of Waters," translated by white men as "alligator." Personal names such as Alligator Man, stories about the monsters which lived in the deep holes of the rivers and sometimes caused swimmers to drown, and other references to the alligator raised questions in the minds of a people who lived in a geographic area void of such creatures.

The Osage (Lower Missouri Sioux) are one of the few Siouan peoples to have an oral tradition that begins in the East. Their stories indicate that after crossing the Appalachian Mountains the Siouan tribes followed the valleys of the New River and the Big Sandy to the Ohio River. According to the oral historians, the nation spent time at the forks of the Allegheny and Monogahela Rivers and at the falls of the Ohio, near present day Louisville. The nation allegedly began to separate here.

Those who did not remain in the Ohio territory were said to have followed its waters until they reached the Missouri River. Here another division took place, with some tribes moving up the mouth of the Missouri while others were said to have followed the Mississippi north.

It also seems very probable that a partial division occurred near the mouth of the Illinois and Rock Rivers, with the remaining tribes moving north into Wisconsin. It is also possible that they followed the Mississippi north to where it met the Wisconsin. Then, following the Wisconsin River, they reached the Fox River where they spread out throughout Green Bay and the surrounding region.

Another Siouan cousin of the Crow, the Winnebago, whose origin story places their creation in the Green Bay area, recall that a separation of the greater nation took place after having reached the Lake Michigan territory. The fragmentary account relates that:

> ...on Lake Michigan the tribe was so large that each clan had its own chief and a general chief presided over the whole tribe. After a while it became so hard to obtain food that a band went south. They never returned. These are now in the Southeast. Some of them are in

Missouri and some in Iowa. Band after band kept moving away until only one was left, the present Winnebago.

It may be at this point, somewhere near Green Bay, Wisconsin that the Crow people broke away from their Siouan relatives and continued one of the most incredible migrations in history.

THE HOKAN-SIOUAN STOCK: THE SIOUAN FAMILY
WISSLER-KLUCKHOLM

Dakota Tribes	*Lower Missouri*
Eastern Dakota	Iowa
Santee Dakota	Missouri
Teton Dakota	Osage
Blackfeet Sioux	Quapaw
Brule	Ponca
Hunkpapa	Omaha
Miniconjou	Oto
Oglala	Kansas
Sans Arc	
Two Kettle	
Yankton Dakota	

Upper Missouri	*Virginia-North Carolina*
Mandan	Saponi
Hidatsa	Tutelo
Crow	Monacan
	Manahoac
	Catawba

Others

Assiniboin
Winnebago
Biloxi

Joe Medicine Crow of Lodge Grass, Montana, became the historian of the Crow Nation in 1948. He has done more than any other person to trace migration of his people to their current homeland. As a youth, Medicine Crow became interested in traditional stories and legends. He was fortunate to grow up among so many aged story tellers who had connections with the distant past. Starting in his youth, Joe recorded the stories of over one hundred old-timers on everything from the Crow migration to the Custer expedition against the Sioux and Cheyenne. In his own words, Medicine Crow has tried to use "oral history, the writings of early explorers and trappers, and archaeology to put together an accurate migration story."

What follows is essentially the Crow migration story as related by Medicine Crow to students at the annual Big Woods/Big Plains Seminar held in Stillwater, Minnesota in April, 1987.

The Crow were woodland Indians who planted corn and squash when they lived south of Lake Superior and east of Lake Michigan. They hunted the game and enjoyed the life in a land filled with a variety of wild life, fruits, berries, and nuts. But one year, according to legend, the rains did not come. The hot winds began blowing continuously and soon the green earth was parched to brown. The corn and squash could not be planted. The buffalo retreated and the tribe became hungry.

The men of the tribe were then called together to decide what to do. They decided to send teams of 14 men to each of the four directions in search of game. When the men returned from the north, they reported that they saw nothing. It was the same for those who had gone to the east and to the south. But when the men from the west returned, they had brought back buffalo meat with each man carrying all that he could.

After all had eaten, the men were asked to make their report. They said that many days to the west they finally came out of the woods. There they found many buffalo on the open plains and meadows. There was good grass and good water. After hearing the report, the Chief made the decision to move toward the land of the setting sun. Crow historians believe that the Crow finally caught up with the buffalo somewhere near the present location of St. Paul, Minnesota. From their new home in Minnesota, the Crow people began to wander toward the north. They spent some time ranging

CROW MIGRATION

1=Siouan Land
A=Allegheny
& Monongahela Fork
B=Ohio Falls
C=Missouri River
D=Illinois River

E=Rock River
F=Green Bay Region
G=St. Paul
H=Winnipeg Canada
I=Medicine Lake
J=Heart River

K=Alberta Canada
L=Great Salt Lake
M=New Mexico
N=Arkansas River
2=Promised Place

from northern Minnesota to the Winnipeg area of Canada, a land filled with lakes and bush. Here the Crow lived in two separate groups. In the winter they dwelt in their earthen lodges in meadows of the valley. During the summers some of the people would head west to hunt buffalo, while others farmed.

Oral history is not clear as to exactly why the Crow left their northern home. It may have been that the Cree and the Ojibway had acquired guns from the traders giving them an advantage in warfare.

The two divisions of the tribe now met and decided to head for the Southwest. It was about 1550. When they came to a lake in North Dakota, they decided to stop. They named the lake Medicine Lake, or Sacred Waters. Today, it has interestingly been named Devil's Lake.

Here there was dissension. Some people wanted to return to the north while others wanted to stay or go on. The leaders of the respective divisions were brothers named No-Vitals and Red Scout. They decided to fast, to seek direction from the Great Spirit as to the direction the tribe should take. When they returned from their pilgrimages, Red Scout had an ear of corn. He related that it had been given him by the Great Spirit as his staff of life. Red Scout had been told that he could go anywhere and the corn would grow. He then declared he would live on corn.

No-Vitals had seeds that he had been given by the Great Spirit. He declared that the seeds were not for his body, but for his soul; that he would go to the mountains where the Great Spirit would show him the ways to plant the sacred seeds. He declared that as long as he planted the seeds of tobacco, the people will populate, be healthy and rich, and they will find a good country in which to live.

The people under No-Vitals now packed up their possessions and began to walk toward the west, using travois attached to their dogs to help bear the load. Soon they came to the shores of the Missouri River near its junction with the Heart River. As they looked across the river, they saw a number of earthen lodges which housed a tribe called the Mandan. The Mandans, seeing the arrival of the ancestral Crow, took to their bull boats and paddled toward them. They helped transport the newcomers across the river where they kept and cared for them about a year. After living in the valley along the Missouri for about seven years, the Crow began to move north. They came to the Knife River, a distance of about 17 miles from their former home.

Once more the migrants faced the pressures of starvation. The buffalo had left once again and most of the white-tailed deer were gone. As was the custom, the men once again were sent out to each of the four directions to see what they could find. Only one buffalo had been found. The meat was to be shared so that all might get at least one bite. While No-Vitals was in council with his men, his wife came to him crying that she did not get much meat from the buffalo that was found. No-Vitals, upon hearing the complaint from his wife, called for the crier to notify the people that in the spring, he, No-Vitals, would be moving. Those who wanted to leave with him would be welcome to come along. It was sometime between 1600-1625.

It was a historic day when the people packed. Large dogs and tamed wolves were harnessed to travois. Relatives bade farewells.

No-Vitals and about 400 others faced westward and left. Thus the migration began anew. This migration was perhaps one of the longest and most dramatic of any Indian migration, taking hundreds of years to accomplish and covering thousands of miles over rugged terrain through all kinds of climatic conditions.

When No-Vitals left, he started out fresh, with a brand new tribe without a name as yet. He intentionally decided to travel light. His band became an instant tribe capable of existing as a separate and distinct entity, one motivated with the desire and dream of someday receiving the blessings of the Great Spirit when it reached the right place.

It was the start of a long, dangerous, event-filled migration. No-Vitals and his followers left, moving north up the Missouri River. They passed the Yellowstone and continued on until they reached the Milk River (called the White Bear River by the Crow); they followed the river into Canada where they settled in the Alberta area. They stayed there for a time. Names like Crow Lake, Crow Hill, and Crow Nest today honor their stay in Canada. The Crow still did not have a tribal name. They referred to themselves as "Our Side."

But soon the people recognized a problem with the area. The Chief called the people together and told them that the winters were too long, the snow too deep, and the summers too short. Some Crow were to stay in Canada, but the rest packed and again headed to the south. The exact route is unknown. They may have come down the east side of the Rockies or have followed the plateaus down the west side.

Whichever way they went, they finally came to a great lake, the Great Salt Lake of Utah. It was so long that they could not see the other side as they approached from the north. As they neared the lake they saw stones floating on the water. They stayed for awhile, but the water was too salty to drink. There was salt pan and sage. It was a hostile place. It was no good, so again the Crow packed and headed east.

As they traveled, they came to a place where there was a great hole and the flames blazed high. They called this place "Where There Is A Fire." Perhaps it was a burning coal vein. It may have been somewhere in the present states of Wyoming, Colorado, northern New Mexico, or northern Texas. The people did not like this area so they continued to the east.

Soon they came to a big river they called the Arrowhead River because of the many arrowheads and artifacts they found there. Today it is called the Canadian River of north Texas and Oklahoma. They followed the river until they got to the brush country. Here there were lots of big birds, or turkeys as they are now called. This was still not the place where the Crow wanted to be. They did not like the area because they could not see distant places because of trees.

At this point they were probably in Oklahoma, Arkansas or Missouri. Once again, the decision was made to turn and go in another direction. This time the group headed north and west. Turning westward up the Missouri River, and finally following the North Platte, the wandering tribe continued past the location of modern day city of Casper, Wyoming, and eventually reached the Big Horns.

Here was the promised land, the land sought by No-Vitals and his band when they left Devil's Lake in North Dakota. No-Vitals did not live to see the sacred seeds brought to the right place or the promised land. Perhaps he died in Canada. Legend says he passed the seeds and the sacred ceremony on to Running Coyote, who himself died on the migration, probably in Oklahoma or Arkansas. Running Coyote passed the seeds on to another man, whose name has been lost in time. Paints His Body and Red Fish were, perhaps, chiefs along the way. One Heart was a chief after the Crow had arrived in the new land. He was followed by Raven Face and White Moccasin Top. Along with the sacred seeds, the Crow technique of stampeding buffalo over cliffs, a technique originated by Running Coyote, was also passed on to the generations of the Crow.

And so the Crow Nation, completing a migration from Wisconsin that took them to Canada twice and through the states of Minnesota, North Dakota, Montana, Idaho, Utah, Colorado, New Mexico, Texas, Oklahoma, Arkansas, Missouri, Nebraska, South Dakota, and finally to the right place in northern Wyoming and southern Montana arrived in their promised land. It was about 1700. After 200 years of wandering since leaving Wisconsin, or about one hundred years of travel from the time they left the Hidatsa in North Dakota, the Creator had delivered the Crow.

The Crow started their journey to their new homeland on foot, and they entered their new land on foot. The journey could have only

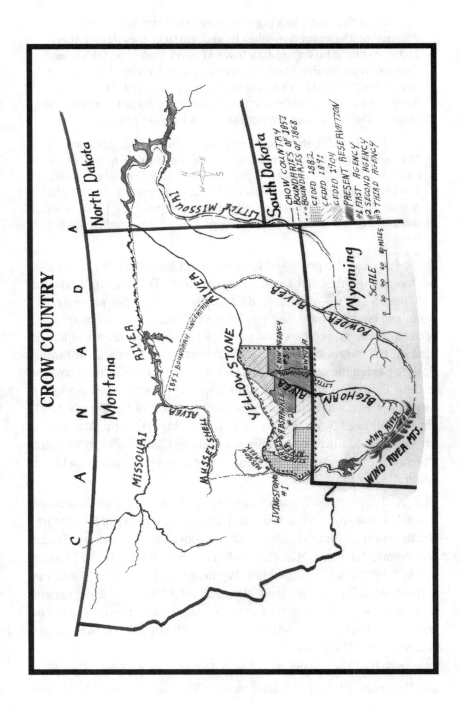

CROW COUNTRY

CANADA

Montana

North Dakota

South Dakota

Wyoming

MISSOURI RIVER

LITTLE MISSOURI

MUSSELSHELL RIVER

YELLOWSTONE RIVER

BIGHORN RIVER

POWDER RIVER

WIND RIVER

WIND RIVER MTS.

1851 BOUNDARY LINE

CROW COUNTRY OF 1851
BOUNDARIES OF 1868
CEDED 1882
CEDED 1891
CEDED 1904
PRESENT RESERVATION
#1 FIRST AGENCY
#2 SECOND AGENCY
#3 THIRD AGENCY

SCALE
0   20   40   60 MILES

LIVINGSTONE #1
#2
CROW AGENCY #3

been accomplished by a determined and proud people. It is little wonder the Crow have always taken pride in their ability to overcome tremendous odds. Needless to say, they admired the same quality in others, including their enemies.

Within 40 years of their arrival in their new land, they acquired the horse. Credit is given to Chief Young White Buffalo, who led a war party near the Green River in northwestern Colorado and successfully returned with the first horses, probably taken from the Shoshonis. Young White Buffalo, who had followed White Moccasin Top as Chief, transformed the Crow from walking to horseback Indians in about 1734. From that time on, the Crow developed their riding abilities, and in a short time were known as some of the greatest horsemen of the plains.

The country that the Crow called their own was later defined in the Treaty of 1851 as an "area bounded on the east by the Powder River, on the west by the headwaters of the Yellowstone River, on the north by the Missouri and Musselshell River, and on the south by the Wind River Mountains." Had the Crow been allotted all of the land within the legal range they claimed, then the Little Missouri and the surrounding region would have been included.

As the Crow explored and hunted this new land, they grew in strength of will and numbers. The feeling they had for the land dreamed of by No-Vitals was expressed by Arapooish (Arapovish), a Crow Chief, to Robert Campbell, of the Rocky Mountain Fur Company in 1832:

> The Crow country is a good country. The Great Spirit has put it exactly in the right place; while you are in it you fare well; whenever you go out of it, whichever way you travel, you fare worse.
>
> If you go to the south you have to wander over great barren plains; the water is warm and bad, and you meet the fever and ague. To the north it is cold; the winters are long and bitter, with no grass; you cannot keep horses there, but travel with dogs. What is country without horses?
>
> On the Columbia they are poor and dirty, paddle about in canoes, and eat fish. Their teeth are worn out; they are always taking fish bones out of their mouths. Fish is a poor food. To the east they

dwell in villages; they live well, but they drink the muddy water of the Missouri. That is bad. A Crow's dog would not drink such water.

About the forks of the Missouri is a fine country — good water, good grass, plenty of buffalo. In summer it is almost as good as the Crow country, but in winter it is cold; the grass is gone, and there is no salt weed for the horses.

The Crow Country is exactly in the right place. It has snowy mountains and sunny plains; all kinds of climates but good things for every season. When the summer heat scorches in the prairie you can draw under the mountains, where the air is sweet and cool, the grass fresh, and the bright streams come tumbling out of the snow banks. There you can hunt the elk, the deer, the antelope, when their skins are fit for dressing; there you will find plenty of white bears and mountain sheep. In the autumn, when your horses are fat and strong from the mountain pastures, you can go down into the plains and hunt for buffalo, or trap the beaver in the streams. And when winter comes, you can take shelter in the woody bottoms along the rivers; there you will find buffalo meat for yourselves, and cottonwood bark for your horses; or you may winter in the Wind River Valley, where there is salt weed in abundance. The Crow Country is exactly in the right place. Everything good is to be found there. There is no country like the Crow Country.

SOURCES

Chapter 1

Buckingham, Cindy, Green, Jan and Stewart, Geneva. *A History Of The Crow Indians Based On Written Sources.* Lodge Grass, Montana: Lodge,Grass Schools, 1972.
Credits individual Crow leaders for their contributions after their arrival in the Big Horn country.

Lawson, Publius V. "The Winnebago Tribe." *Wisconsin Archaeologist,* Vol. 4, No. 3, Milwaukee: Wisconsin Archaeological Society, 1907.
Contains Osage Migration story.

Linderman, Frank B. *Pretty Shield.* Lincoln and London: University of Nebraska, 1932.
Suggests concern about the alligator and Crow origins.

Medicine Crow, Joseph. "The Crow Migration Story." Big Woods/Big Plains lecture series. Stillwater, Minnesota, 6 April 1987.
Videotape consists of the Crow Migration as viewed by Joe Medicine Crow.

Radin, Paul. "The Winnebago Tribe." *Bureau of American Ethnology, 37th Annual Report, 1915-16.* Washington: Government Printing Office, 1923.
Contains Winnebago version of the migration.

"The Crow." *Sheridan Post.* 10 July 1902.
Reprint of Robert Campbell's account of the Crow country.

Wissler, Clark. *Indians of the United States.* Garden City: Doubleday and Company, 1940, revised 1966.
Designates Siouan linguistic family.

II. THEY CAME AS FORETOLD

The white man's arrival in the land of the Crow was not unexpected. Crow visionaries had foretold the coming of the white men years before they actually came to North America. The dreams of the prophets were so accurate that even the clothes worn by and the weapons of the white invader were described. This expected coming of the white man no doubt contributee to the ultimate development of Crow policy toward the newcomer, one of friendship first, then as an ally later.

By the time the first trader-explorers began to enter Crow Territory, they had taken the name "Absaroka." While the word "Absaroka" is obsolete in the dialect used by the Crow today, it still is used by their sister tribe, the Hidatsa. "Abisa" refers to large beaked, and "roka" means its children. The "children of the large beaked bird" were called Crow by the Hidatsa and early French explorer-traders. It cannot be supported conclusively, but the Crow were probably children of the "Raven." Many Siouan groups referred to the Crow as the "Raven" people, and so it would seem the Crow, like so many other Indian nations, acquired a name given to them by others through misinterpretation or misunderstanding.

While certainly others had come before, the La Verendryes brothers were the first whites to leave a record of their entry into the Crow country. Under a French fur trading grant, they met the Crow in 1742, at Tullocks Fork, for the purpose of trading furs. They stayed with the Crow for three weeks, describing them as intelligent, friendly, and most helpful. The La Verendryes called them the "Beaux Hommes," the handsome men. The La Verendryes were to have the last known direct contact with the Crow for nearly 50 years. When they left, the Crow presented the La Verendrys with new horses to replace their tired mounts.

Even before the white man appeared in great numbers, his diseases preceded him. The Crow system of trade included exchange with the Mandans, Hidatsa, Nez Perce, Flatheads, and from time to time the Shoshonis. It may have been through these contacts that the Crow picked up the dreaded smallpox. Because the Crow lived so close together in camps and tepees the disease spread rapidly, reducing the nation from 2,000 to 300 lodges by 1808. Traditional medical practices had no effect on the pox, whose incubation period was from 10 to 14 days. As time progressed, the Crow fought smallpox by dividing the tribe into small groups or families which scattered until the epidemic faded.

In 1805, French Canadian Antoine Larocque appeared with Robert McKenzie, representing the Hudson Bay Fur Company. They traded guns to the Crow for some of the finest horses they had ever seen. While Larocque does not mention that he gave guns to the Crow, tradition says that he did. The Crow already had guns that they had acquired through trade with the Mandan and Hidatsa; however, they were always looking for more and improved weapons to better defend themselves against their enemies who were also trying to improve on their military position.

Larocque contributed to the Crow desire for an improved material culture by giving them presents of glass, combs, axes, feathers, smoking tobacco, rings, knives, paint, flint, gun powder, and musket balls. These gifts were given as an encouragement for the Crow to hunt the beaver, otter, and bear as trade items. Larocque promised that if the Crow traded with the British, then all of their needs would be met. Whatever agreement might have been reached, the British made no attempt to carry out their end of the bargain.

Lewis and Clark came to the Crow country after returning from their venture to the west coast. On July 18, 1806, they noted smoke signals that they believed to be from the Crow. Three days later, the expedition lost some 24 horses. This was to be the only contact Lewis and Clark had with the Crow.

In October, 1807, Fort Lisa, a small cabin, was established at the mouth of the Bighorn River by Manuel Lisa and John Colter, representing the Missouri Fur Company out of St. Louis. In 1809, Thomas James set up a trading post on the three forks of the Missouri. A year later the post was abandoned, and by 1811 Fort Lisa had also folded. Constant battles with the Blackfeet and wars between the

Blackfeet and the Crow were, no doubt, responsible for the demise of the forts. There were no major trade attempts into the Crow territory in 1812, due in part to the great war being fought between the "whites of across the water" and the "new Americans."

By the 1820s, warfare between the Cheyenne and the Crow was increasing primarily because of the pressure the Cheyenne were feeling from other tribes who were moving into their territory, which in turn caused the Cheyenne to infringe on Crow land. Trappers and military representatives who visited the Crow found them willing to help in any way they could, including protecting them against other tribes, especially the Blackfeet, Sioux, and Cheyenne.

In 1825, William Ashley, who later founded the Rocky Mountain Fur Company, perfected the rendezvous, thus allowing the trappers to spend an entire year trapping in a region. While the fur company saved money by not having to build, maintain, and stock a post, the Crow had to do more and more care-taking as the population of trappers increased. 1824 saw the creation of the Bureau of Indian Affairs within the Department of War. The Department of War was especially concerned with Indian trade with the British. They also were wary of potential Indian wars and/or Indian alliances with foreign powers, and thought it would be nice to keep peace in the west so that the trappers could do their work. As a result, the U.S. Government sent General Henry Atkinson and Agent Major Benjamin O'Fallon, along with a military escort, to negotiate treaties of "friendship" with various tribes, including the Crow. As Atkinson moved up the Missouri, he found the Crow visiting the Mandan. Atkinson's first contact with the Crow proved to be controversial and potentially dangerous.

With one of the Crow warriors was a half-breed woman and child. Atkinson insisted that she be freed from the relationship with the Crow warrior. It should be pointed out that she was not in bondage, but was married to the man, by Crow custom, and with him of her own free will. When one of the Crow leaders began to give Atkinson a hard time, O'Fallon finally became so upset that he hit the Crow man on the head with the butt of his pistol. The Crow made no sound as he continued to stare with wonderment at the offender.

Upon hearing of the incident, the Council of Chiefs met to discuss with great anger the ill treatment of a fellow warrior by the white man. Cooler heads prevailed, and the incident seemed to be resolved, until the Crow noticed that the military visitors were setting up their camp with their big guns pointing in the direction of the Crow. When the Crow tried to block the guns' placement, a scuffle broke out in which, Arapooish [Sore Belly], one of the two major leaders of the Crow, was tripped. Very upset, Arapooish went off by himself and sang his medicine song to the Thunderbird. The results of his meditation had a devastating effect. A hail storm of some magnitude rained down on all those encamped with the Mandan. While the storm destroyed the Mandan crops in their fields, it had a calming effect on both parties negotiating the Treaty of Friendship.

Arapooish was not happy and probably always afterward had an ill feeling and mistrust for the whites. Although he would not sign the treaty himself, Long Hair, a chief of equal authority, did sign the agreement. It may be that Arapooish did not greatly resist the signing because he and his advisors remembered the ancient visions, and recalled the prophecy of Old Spotted Horse. Some time before the coming of Lewis and Clark in the late 1700s, Spotted Horse had dreamed that the Crow "would see the whites come in great numbers, be their friends, help them in any way that you can..." No matter how this white man might act, Crow leadership believed that he might be useful, if not now, then later. The Crow were well aware that in "1824 the Sioux, Cheyenne, and Arapahoe, had made an agreement designed to conquer the buffalo country of the Crow." The Crow would need allies.

In effect, the Treaty of Friendship of 1825 placed the Crow Nation in the position of recognizing the U.S. Government as a superior authority. The Crow agreed to remain in the territorial confines of the United States, to submit to United States trade regulation, and not to seek private revenge, but rather to go to the proper authorities if problems arose. Even though it would have been impossible during these times to enforce such an agreement, it set the tone for United States-Crow treaties of the future.

During the winter of 1830, a war party of Sioux stole 150 head of horses from the Crow. The Crow gave chase for some time, and then finally decided to return to camp. Twenty-three young warriors, after some discussion, decided to exercise their option to continue the chase of the thieves. Finally, after several hours without success, they, too, decided to return home and to seek revenge another day. What they didn't realize was that they had been seen by the Sioux who surrounded them that night as they camped. When the fighting erupted, the greatly outnumbered Crow were driven into a gully where all 23 of the young men were annihilated. With this in mind, the Crow viewed the building of Fort Cass in 1832, on the former Fort Lisa site, as an opportunity to equip themselves for the increasing raids and warfare with the Sioux and Cheyenne.

As the traders began to increase in numbers and the wars continued, the artists and writers began to show up to paint their pictures and describe Indian life as they saw it. George Catlin gave his impressions:

> As far as my travels have yet led me into the Indian country. I have more than realized my former predictions that those Indians who could be found most entirely in a state of nature, with the least knowledge of civilized society, would be found to be the most cleanly in their persons, elegant dress and manners, and enjoying life to the greatest perfection. Of such tribes, perhaps the Crow and Blackfeet stand first.

Catlin believed that the Crow "surpassed the world in skin dressing; they made the most beautiful lodges of any tribe on the continent;" and he was most impressed with "the length of their hair, and their tall, elegant, well formed figures which they carried with ease and grace."

During the winter of 1832, the Comanches were battling the Cheyenne. The Cheyenne, fresh from defeat, entered into the Crow land where they noticed about 30 lodges camped along the Cheyenne River in Wyoming. The ensuing Cheyenne attack destroyed almost everyone in the village. Those who escaped notified Chief Arapooish who was visiting and trading with the Flatheads.

Arapooish returned with revenge on his mind. He gathered together some 600 fighting men determined to find the Cheyenne. After many days of travel, the Crow discovered the Cheyenne camped near the Arkansas River in Colorado near the Kansas border.

Arapooish divided his command into two groups under himself and Little White Bear. When the Cheyenne camp was quiet, Arapooish sent in seven men to drive the horses from the village. In the confusion, the two groups surrounded the village and "laid on" a devastating defeat. Two hundred Cheyenne fighting men were killed, and 270 women and children were taken prisoners. Only five Crow warriors lost their lives.

Just as the Crow were starting to move for home, they met a wagon train coming up the Arkansas River. Some members of the train had smallpox. Even though the leaders of the wagon train tried to warn the Crow contingent, it was of no avail. Before the slow moving war party reached home, some members of the Crow party were coming down with the disease. The attack of smallpox took the lives of half the Crow nation.

Arapooish blamed the whites for this destruction of his people. With some difficulty, he gathered people together and explained to them his plan of revenge. He hoped to accomplish several goals. He would get at the whites by taking over Fort McKenzie, which belonged to the American Fur Company. He would gain needed supplies from the fort for his people, and at the same time deny his enemy, the Blackfeet, the guns and ammunition they were obtaining from the fort to use against the Crow.

The battle plan was unique. He divided his people into three groups, who set up their camp surrounding the fort. The goal was to starve the fort, under the command of Alexander Culbertson, into surrender. For 10 days nothing happened; then a single cannon shot was fired from the fort into the Crow camp. The Crow did not return the fire, and no one appeared to have been injured. Shortly after this incident, the Blackfeet returned from a venture in Canada and the Crow retreated, primarily because they were facing fire from both the front and the rear.

The Crow were very committed to the keeping of personal vows. Arapooish had stated that should his siege of the fort fail, he would leave his body in the home of the Blackfeet. The Crow attacked, killing several of the enemy who entrenched themselves in a natural fortification. Arapooish wanted to charge them, but his soldiers argued that the Blackfeet were too well protected. After seemingly agreeing, Arapooish kneed his horse at full speed toward the Blackfeet. He was successful in killing one of the enemy with his lance, but died in battle as he had wanted, having been shot numerous times with enemy arrows. His body was dressed, wrapped, and placed in a tree.

By the 1840s, times were changing for the Crow. The Crow continued to be one nation and one people, but more and more they began to separate into three major groups. It seems the separation made it easier to find adequate food supplies. The "Main Camp," as they called themselves, would continue to have the greatest numbers and would spend most of their time in the Montana-Wyoming territory near the Big Horn Mountains. The whites called the Main Camp, the "Mountain Crow." Another major group called the "River Crow" lived near the upper Missouri River. The third group, the "Kicked in the Bellies," spent some time in the Little Bighorn and Powder River valleys, but gradually moved over the mountains into the Wind River area. The Crow caught the smallpox once again in 1848, and in 1849 the flu struck, killing some 600.

The last rendezvous recorded was in 1837. The emphasis in trade was moving from the scarce beaver to the buffalo. For the Crow, this meant that there were fewer white trappers to deal with. It also meant that there were fewer posts in and around the Crow country with which to trade. The result found the Crow traveling further and further to trade for items which they desired and found useful as they integrated them into their culture. Increased travel to the remaining posts, such as Fort Union on the Missouri, brought the Crow into greater contact with their enemies. As the pressure of intruding tribes increased, the concept of warfare was beginning to change from one of just attempting to acquire war honors to one of protecting Crow territory and preserving the nation.

In 1849, the Bureau of Indian Affairs (BIA) was moved from the Department of War to the Department of Interior. With the opening of the Oregon Trail in 1847, the California Gold Rush of 1849, and the increasing travel west by the covered wagons, the B.I.A. sought to create a reservation policy to establish boundaries among the tribes and gain their promise of peaceful relationships with the new white and Indian invaders.

In 1851, members of the Sioux, Cheyenne, Arapaho, Shoshone, Arikara, Assiniboine, Atsina, and Crow nations were called together on Horse Creek, near Fort Laramie, Wyoming. Perhaps the largest Indian gathering ever of over 10,000 people met with government representatives Tom Fitzpatrick, Jim Bridger, and Robert Campbell.

The agreements reached provided that in return for protecting white travelers, the Crow were to be granted 38,532,174 acres of land with the defined boundaries mentioned earlier. In addition, the Crow were to receive food supplies amounting to $50,000 per year "forever." In 1852, the United States Senate eliminated the word "forever" and substituted instead "10 years." The treaty further provided that military posts and roads could be built through the territory. The gathered nations agreed to cease hostilities against each other and to make an effective and lasting peace. Big Robber of the Crow signed the treaty, but Rottentail, a leader of equal authority, did not attend the gathering. It should be noted that no one for the Crow signed the amended Treaty of 1852 that had reduced the annuities promised the Crow. While the treaty had given definition to Crow territory, it had little or no effect on the peoples involved. Other Indian nations continued their encroachment, and war parties on all sides operated as they had traditionally done in the past. It was under these historical circumstances that White-Man-Runs-Him was born into the world of the Crow, into a world of change and uncertainty.

SOURCES

Chapter II

Barstow, L. T. (ed.) *Journal of Francois Antoine Larocque: From Assiniboine to the Yellowstone*. 1805. Ottawa: Government Printing Bureau, 1910. *Early white contact with the Crow.*

Catlin, George. *North American Indian,* Vol. 1. New York: Dover University Inc., 1973. *Impressions of the Crow.*

Ewers, John (ed.) *Five Tribes of the Upper Mississippi.* Norman: University of Oklahoma, 1961. *Statistical information.*

Heidenreich, Conrad. "A History of the Crow of Montana." Unpublished Thesis. University of Oregon, 1974. *History of the Crow.*

Medicine Crow, Joseph. Personal interview.
17 June 1990. *Crow prophesy and advice of Spotted Horse.*
11 June 1989. *1824 Sioux-Cheyenne agreement, Crow battles and history, death of Arapooish.*

III. IN THE TRADITIONAL WAY

White-Man-Runs-Him was raised in the generation that would be considered the last of the traditional way. He was born near the present-day town of Edgar, Montana, a member of the Mountain Crow, Big Lodge Clan. In just what year he was born, no one will probably ever know. Some military records give his birth date as 1854, but since he could not speak English, and since he had no experience with the white concept of time, it is likely that the military that signed him on as a scout helped determine the date of his birth. His application for pension filled out on April 5, 1922 ,shows that he was born in 1855. Several census reports show, however, that he was born in the spring of 1858, and many of his descendants agree.

Winona Plenty Hoops, a granddaughter, raised for a time by White-Man-Runs-Him, stated that his war shirt, "worn at the Custer fight, was very small." She therefore concluded that he was 18 at the time of the Little Big Horn, and not 22, as often suggested by a number of historians. Since he grew up to be a fairly big man, "unable to wear the small shirt," Winona reasons and believes that the 1858 birth date makes sense because a great deal of growth in height and breadth of shoulders does not usually occur after 22 years of age.

White-Man-Runs-Him's father was called Bull-Chief, a famous warrior who had fulfilled the goals of Crow culture by accomplishing many war deeds. He was known and remembered for rushing an enemy fortification and taking the protective enemy medicine pipe that was extending from the barricade. On another occasion he dashed into a battle without apparent concern and counted coup in a situation in which no one else dared to follow. His name,"Bull Chief," had been acquired when he attacked an enemy, secured his weapons, then counted coup by striking him.

Bull-Chief was married five times during his lifetime. Little is known of Bull-Chief's wives other than they bore him six children. White-Man-Runs-Him was the only child of the marriage between Bull-Chief and Offers-Her-Only-Child.

White-Man-Runs-Him (Photo courtesy of the Newberry Library, Chicago)

When Offers-Her-Only-Child was about to deliver White-Man-Runs-Him she went into a tepee with a midwife. Inside the tepee was a bed of buffalo hide with the hair turned up. Two sticks were placed at the head of her pillow. Buffalo robes were rolled up and placed against the two stakes so that when she kneeled, her elbows would have a place to rest. Potions from roots and horned toads were rubbed on her back to hasten delivery. A special drink made from plants was then consumed. When she was ready, Offers-Her-Only-Child knelt, took hold of the two sticks and delivered. When White-Man-Runs-Him was born, as was the custom, three fingers breadth of the naval cord was cut off. Songs were sung as the baby was greased with a mixture including red paint. He was then sprinkled with fine clay and wrapped in soft buckskin. No males observed the delivery, but when the midwife left the lodge, payment was waiting by the door. It is believed by the descendants of White-Man-Runs-Him that payment was made in the form of a fine horse, as was often the case in those days.

Each day after his birth, White-Man-Runs-Him was bathed in cold water from a nearby stream to toughen him. On the fourth day after his birth, his father, grandfather, or a very important person was invited in to name him. It is only known that in the case of White-Man-Runs-Him, he was given his name by a warrior of great distinction, whose vision or positive experience determined the name. Incense made from wild carrot root was smoked by the namer or godfather who lifted the youngster four times toward to sky. The godfather recounted his vision or experience that determined the name he was bestowing on the child; then he prayed that the baby would be strong and brave, always walking in the firm path. The birth name given to White-Man-Runs-Him was *B-She-es-chay-e-coo-sis*, meaning Albino-Buffalo-Turns-Around, or White-Buffalo-That-Turns-Around.

A young man's name might be changed more than once during his lifetime in accordance with Crow tradition: "From ridiculous acts of the father's clan relatives names were frequently applied, in the belief that these would excite the merriment of the spirits and be spoken of among them, thus causing the bearers to become great." Since the Crow enjoyed nicknames, it was not surprising that White-

Man-Runs-Him was given his name by his "joking clansmen" after an incident in the life of a clan uncle. It seems that one day, his clan uncle was with a small group of Crow somewhere along the Missouri River. Noticing the cabin of a trapper, the group moved toward the cabin with the hope of getting some coffee. The trapper produced his gun, and it soon became obvious that he was neither going to give or sell coffee to the Crow. As the angry trapper fired over the heads of the young men, White-Man-Runs-Him's clan uncle began to run. In fact, he ran all the way back to the main Crow encampment, over a mile away. Thus, "Chased-By-A-White-Man" was added to his name. The joking clansmen passed the name White-Man-Runs-Him on to Albino-Buffalo-Turns-Around at about age 10, and he would carry the name White-Man-Runs-Him until he gave it away near the end of his life.

A number of historians who have written about the name of White-Man-Runs-Him have quoted Dr. W. A. Petzoldt, a former minister of the Lodge Grass Baptist Church who knew White-Man-Runs-Him quite well. Petzoldt, who gave the address at White-Man-Runs-Him's funeral, said that he was given his name by a war chief who chose an incident in his grandfather's life for the naming. Petzoldt declared further that when White-Man-Runs-Him's grandfather was young, he and several other Crow were "ambushed" by a greater number of whites "who apparently were out to kill these Crow." Recognizing the dangerous situation they were in, the grandfather "decided that his 'best ammunition' was a pair of good legs and swift moccasins. He escaped in good time which gave rise to the name White-Man-Runs-Him." Perhaps time had confused Petzoldt when he recalled the story of the naming.

Generally, White-Man-Runs-Him did not speak a great deal about his childhood. He told one interviewer that his childhood was a normal Crow experience. For White-Man-Runs-Him that meant that by six moons, he was placed in a cradleboard, and soon after was riding behind his mother on horseback. His mother had her legs tied just above the knees and around the horses neck to prevent her and the young child from falling off and being injured. By four snows, White-Man-Runs-Him was learning to take care of himself on foot and horseback.

In the Crow way, he was not beaten as a child when discipline seemed necessary. As was common among many plains tribes, he was never instructed to do something, but rather he learned through his own experiences, even if at times they proved to be negative ones. Throwing water at him was a means of discipline when his parents were annoyed or disgusted. Crying was frowned upon by the Crow because it might draw the attention of a potential or real enemy to the camp. If a youngster cried or whined too much, then he was placed on his back, and water was poured up his nose. The next time a parent called for water, the child usually stopped crying.

For White-Man-Runs-Him, as for all children, games were real-life situations in the miniature that taught important cultural values. His youth was filled with play designed to educate and prepare him to fulfill his future role as an adult Crow warrior. Plenty Coup recalled that in play all boys are much alike. "Their hearts are young, and they let them sing."

He was taught at a very young age that he must learn his lessons well, for those who fail would not survive the times ahead. White-Man-Runs-Him said that he was first taught to run because it was key in both hunting and war. In the Crow way, it seemed everyone was a teacher, including his father, grandfathers, uncles, and a variety of interested educators.

He often remembered good games, when a teacher would instruct a group of young boys to strip, except for their moccasins, and then attempt to catch a butterfly. If he caught the butterfly, then he rubbed the wings over his heart so that he could gain the grace and swiftness of the butterfly. White-Man-Runs-Him loved to run. He often challenged others to race against him, and if he lost the race, then he challenged his opponent to yet another longer race. If he lost again, he called for yet another race of increased distance, "for he knew that he was long winded and would usually win the race in the end."

For White-Man-Runs-Him, the bow and arrow was life itself. The Grandchild Myth of the Crow tells of an old woman who wished to determine the sex of a young intruder. To find out, she placed in her garden a bow and arrow along with a shiny stick and ball. When the bow and arrow were found missing, she assumed the intruder to be a boy.

For as long as could be remembered, members of the Crow tribe sharpened their knives and scrapers at this spot by pulling the tools against the rock. (Dennis Harcey and Joe Medicine Crow pictured.)

White-Man-Runs-Him liked to recall that "until I was 15 years of age, together with my boy playmates, we trained with bows and arrows." He often talked in later years about shooting buffalo calves as a youth. This he said, "gave me practice for two purposes, protection and support."

His first bow was given to him by his father. It was made of cedar and backed with sinew to give it strength. It was his pride and joy. The arrows at first were blunted on the end, but by the time he was 10 years of age, points replaced the dull ends. Almost from the time he acquired his first bow, White-Man-Runs-Him was making his own arrows with his own personal mark and with the tribal mark being placed in an appropriate place.

White-Man-Runs-Him never forgot that the first thing he was taught to do was to fire for distance. Before he became concerned about accuracy, he had to achieve distance. He enjoyed the competition of two groups of boys firing at a bundle of grass tied with willow bark at a distance of some 40 feet. For variety, the target was sometimes tossed in the air, and in other cases buffalo chips were rolled on the ground and shot at. The victors were able to claim some of the losers' arrows, while the poorest shots were relegated to tossing or rolling the targets. There was much incentive to improve marksmanship, and White-Man-Runs-Him was among the best.

He often said that once he achieved distance and accuracy, then he began to work on speed in shooting. Speed was necessary for those who were to be the most successful on the hunt and in combat. Several arrows were held in the left hand with the points down so that when the right hand drew them, the left hand would not be spiked by the points. In war, the arrows were sometimes held in the mouth to enhance speed when shooting rapid fire.

The practice with the bow from early youth developed a powerful arm and a strong wrist which were needed to drive an arrow forward and downward through a buffalo's paunch. The shot might not stop the buffalo in its tracks, but would be mortal, forcing it to drop out of the herd and die shortly thereafter. White-Man-Runs-Him often declared that the bow was far superior to the muzzle loader that many Crow used because it was next to impossible to load the weapon on a moving horse.

White-Man-Runs-Him told Dixon he "always had an ambition to do more than the best man in the camp could do. I would bring home a buffalo or I would not go home. My folks rejoiced, believing that they had a good boy to help support the family."

He often related how in his youth the camps would be moved every 10 days. In this way the tribal health was maintained, in part because the garbage smells would, over time, become repulsive. The movement of a camp was happy and exciting for the young. When the crier announced the movement, the boys would catch the horses that the herders had brought in. They would then help pack the horses and the travois they were to pull. As the procession moved through the mountains or across the plains, the young males were told to stay with the women and the loaded cargo.

As he grew older, White-Man-Runs-Him remembered the thrill of showing off as he raced back and forth past the women and girls. He was well "aware of the discussions among the girls of how handsome and or how brave the riders were. If on our way to the camp we came across game, such as a rabbit, we shot it with our arrow, broiled it and ate it for fun. When we got to the new camp, we would all praise one boy for some deed that he had performed on the way and then we would all sing and dance. That boy's folks would give all us boys a dish of pemmican for the good deed he had performed." White-Man-Runs-Him told of crossing wide streams, and how he and the other boys would measure the width of the river, and compete with each other to see who could swim the stream without stopping. He told Dixon, "I am telling you now what I did to build myself up to the the man I am now."

For White-Man-Runs-Him, swimming was great fun. In all seasons he and his friends were in the rivers before the sun was up. His teachers were tough, often sending the young boys into the rivers to swim among the ice floats. They were told that this would teach them to take care of their bodies and to toughen them for the life to come. In the winter, they were told, the buffalo runners rubbed their hands with sand and snow to prevent their fingers from stiffening when they used the bow.

White-Man-Runs-Him often related, with great pleasure, stories of how a clan uncle, grandfather, or some other instructor would call out, "Follow me." The boys would then chase after the teacher who would do a flip into the water. If any boy failed to do the flip properly, he was thrown in to the stream and dunked. It was part of the ritual for the boys to slap their joints and muscles with the flat of a beaver's tail until their skin burned. "'Teach us your power in the water, O Beaver,' we said, making our skins smart with the tail."

The young men and boys of the Crow emulated their fathers by talking of warriors and war. They had their own leaders, many of whom became chiefs when they reached the adult world. The adult leaders of the young were wise and never neglected the young or failed to keep before them deeds done by the outstanding warriors and leaders of the tribe. The adult leaders praised the young men for their good deeds and efforts and said little that might tend to belittle a youth or cause him to become discouraged or depressed. The program was very thorough, and any boy who failed at any lesson received more care and instruction until he had accomplished all that he could.

The young were often referred to by their teachers as "Magpies," meaning mischievous, persistent ones. White-Man-Runs-Him described when he and his friends were called by a teacher: "Fifteen or 20 of us boys would go out to the river and daub ourselves up with mud, and so disguise ourselves that no one in camp would know us. Then we would take [steal in the manner of the wolves] jerked buffalo beef that the women had hung up around the camp to dry."

The boys were being trained to steal horses, and the meat they were taking was referred to as horses by their teachers. The young man could gain a pretend coup for stealing or "cutting" a horse, as it was called by the Crow. When the boys returned to the teacher with the stolen meat, each successful coup was complimented, then the successful boys were given a stick which symbolized that they had the honor of counting coup. White-Man-Runs-Him said that when this was done, they went out of sight and had a feast of the meat. None of the boys were caught on this particular raid because they were covered or disguised with mud. Sometimes on such raids they covered themselves with the skin of a wolf they had borrowed from a father or relative, perhaps without their knowledge. If caught on one of these missions, the captured youth would not tell who his accomplices were. Sometimes the offenders were caught by the old women who dragged them to the water where their faces were washed and they were identified. After it had been determined who the culprit was, he was usually given the meat he had taken; however, no coup could be claimed by the captured.

Another favorite activity was wrestling, which usually took place among boys of the same age and size. White-Man-Runs-Him recalled "if a boy downed me three or four times, I kept up the practice of wrestling until I had more strength. Then I could throw this boy and I was satisfied."

The Crow learned how to ride well at an early age. "We were also taught the management of horses," which, of course, included the Crow philosophy that both horses and rider must come to understand each other. "Horse and rider must fight together as one and fast together as one. They must know each other's hearts and desires so that they become as brothers. The horse has a soul; he understands. Look in his eyes and you can see his soul. When we were quite small boys, we would go out hunting horses and bring back a dog and call it a horse, such was the emphasis of our youth."

Girls and boys often played together during the childhood of White-Man-Runs-Him. At about 10 years of age, they pretended to move camp, marry one another, celebrate the return of a war party, and in general play the adult roles observed in their environment. In the winter, toboggans were built of eight to 10 buffalo ribs, which were attached together and covered with rawhide.

Sometimes just for the fun of it, White-Man-Runs-Him and his friends would venture out at night to steal the two outside lodge poles of some family's home. If the lodge residents were able to give chase and were successful in catching the thieves, then the pranksters were made to forfeit their blankets to the offended party. If the youngsters were not captured, they retreated to a safe spot, laughed, and made sport of their successful efforts.

White-Man-Runs-Him often spoke of the fact that during his youth, he watched what the old people did. Then when he grew up, he went forth equipped. He observed the adults playing many of the same games as the children, and he watched them playing games reserved for adults. They were great gamblers, betting headdresses, beadwork and other possessions. One game that had great appeal to the adults was the guessing game played with two people or two groups facing each other. The object was to guess which hand held the elk's tooth or shell. Sometimes the person who held the objects moved them from hand to hand under a buffalo robe to complicate the guess. The game was played with great fanfare, and often when two groups were pitted against each other, a pipe smoker sat behind each group. Drums were beaten and songs sung by either the participants or the audience to show encouragement or give support. Each player could appeal to his protector if he desired. Poor guesses would be jeered and mock songs sung to ridicule the losers.

Another favorite game was the mock hunting game which consisted of attempting to throw a 42 inch dart with two plumed prongs through a nine inch rolling hoop. This game demanded highly skilled participants and is still enjoyed to this day.

Education for White-Man-Runs-Him, besides play, consisted of stories told around the campfires in the morning or evening or some special event. Such stories might be told by an older adult, parent, or relative. The stories emphasized Crow cultural traditions and history, thus giving rise to a rich oral tradition. White-Man-Runs-Him often recounted the favorite stories of his youth:

> In early days we had nothing except the skins of animals. We used the buffalo hide or the deer hide for a breech-clout. For a bucket we used the tripe of the buffalo. After thoroughly cleaning it, we would hang it up on the branch of a tree, full of water, and drink out of it.

> The white people came long before I was born, but when I first remembered the white man I thought he was very funny.

> Going back to the days when we had no horses, we would see the buffalo on the plains; we then surrounded them, driving them as we did so near the edge of some steep precipice. When we got buffalo up near the edge of the precipice, we would all wave our blankets and buffalo robes and frighten the buffalo, and they would run off the steep place, falling into the valley below, one on top of another. Of course, the undermost animals were killed. Then we would go down and get them and take away the meat.

The Crow used a variety of techniques to drive buffalo over cliffs which they referred to as the "buffalo jump." According to tradition, "Old Man Coyote," the cultural teacher of the Crow, taught the Crow the technique of "tricking buffalo" over embankments.

Joe Medicine Crow explained one buffalo jump technique used by the Crow from 1650 through the time of White-Man-Runs-Him, and until the buffalo days were gone:

> The night before the drive and jump, a council would be held and the participants were selected, some to drive the herd from the rear and a few to haze the jumpoff point. Sometimes dogs were used on the drive. A Medicine Man was also asked to officiate the undertaking. Early in the morning, this Medicine Man would stand on the edge of the upper cliff, facing up the ridge. He would take a pair of bison hind quarters and, pointing the feet along a

line of stones, would sing his sacred songs and call council upon the Great Spirit to make the operation a success. After this invocation, the Medicine Man would give the two head drivers a pouch of incense. As the two head drivers, and their helpers headed up the ridge along the line of stones, they would stop and burn incense on the ground, repeating the process four times.

When the two groups reached the top, they formed a line and started down the ridge. All the animals along the ridge would be chased downhill, including buffalo, deer, wapiti, bighorn sheep, and even small animals.

The mysterious thing about this is that the animals would come to the line where incense was burned and bolt back into the ridge area. Apparently there was little or no deployment of hazers along the incense line except near the cliff. Here the rock piles were higher, larger, and closer together to afford some protection for the hazers.

Incense placed near the rocks guided the buffalo over the jump.

While sitting around the fire in the evening, White-Man-Runs-Him enjoyed talking about the days gone by. Dixon quoted him speaking about the use of dogs:

> The Indians found some dogs on the prairie. After they got the dogs they would fasten a pole on either side of the dogs with a tanned hide fastened between the poles, and the Indians would put their trappings, their meat, and their papooses on this hide stretched between the poles. In that way they moved from place to place, the dog carrying the utensils of the camp. We called it a travois. One day when we were moving, the dog who was carrying a baby in the travois saw a deer and ran after it. He went over a bank and carried the baby with him, and finally came back without the baby.

White-Man-Runs-Him liked to tell of an earlier time when his tribe counted the dead on the battlefield by placing sticks by the deceased. When all the sticks had been placed they were gathered up and tallied:

> We count by fixing events in our mind. We have a brain and a heart, and we commit to memory an event, and then we say Chief So and So died when we broke camp on the Big Horn, and So and So were married when we had the big buffalo hunt in the snow. Or we had a big fight with the Sioux when our tepees were placed in a ring in the bend of the Yellowstone River. We dated our time from these events.

A long-time favorite story of White-Man-Runs-Him was a Crow tradition and told around the campfire of every lodge. The story was called "Old Man Coyote." In the words of White-Man-Runs-Him:

> Before the white man came the coyote used to roam over all the land. The Old Man Coyote took the little coyotes he picked up on the prairies and called them his little brothers. The little coyote was such a sly animal that he would always be up to something. The Old Man Coyote said: "We are alone: let us make man." He said: "Go and bring me some mud so that I can make a man, so that we can be together." The Old Man Coyote took the mud and put it together, and put hair on it, and set it up on the ground, and said: "There is a man." The little coyote said: "Make some more." And the Old Man Coyote made four — two were women and two were men. The Old Man sized them up and said they were good, and so he made a whole lot more. Old Man Coyote said: "It is good that we live together, and I want you to open

each other's eyelids. Now, if you stay together and are good to each other, you will be happy and you will increase in numbers."

Old Man Coyote was our creator. Old Man Coyote said to these people whom he had made: "This is your land; live here, eat of the fruit of the trees, drink of the rivers, hunt the game, and have a good time."

From that we believe that the white people had nothing to do with the land — it belonged to the Indian. This story, told to our people so many times, and told to me since I can remember, led me to believe when I came to know and understand that this land was wholly ours, and belonged entirely to the Indians. Old Man Coyote, after he created man and woman, did not have anything to do, so he made a bow and arrow. He took the flint for the arrowhead, and with it he killed the buffalo. Then he gave the bow and arrow to the Indian and said to him: "This is your weapon." The people whom Old Man Coyote created had no knife, so he took the shoulder blade of the buffalo and made it into a knife. These people whom Old Man Coyote had created roamed round over the land and they found a mule. It was a great mule with great ears, and when they brought it home the people were all afraid of it. They all gathered around the mule, staring in amazement at him, and said: "What kind of an animal is this? It is a dangerous animal." Just then the mule struck up his ears, and let out an awful cry, just such a cry as only the mule can make. The people all ran away as hard as they could go, scared almost to death, except one Indian, who fell flat on the earth — too scared to run. And finally the people called this man, "Not-Afraid-of-the-Mule." And in this way we learned how to name our Indians.

SOURCES

Chapter III

Curtis, Edward S. *The North American Indian.* Vol. III. New York: Johnson Reprint Corporation, 1908.
Deals with Crow names.

Department of the Interior Bureau of Pensions. Records contained by Bishop Henry Whipple . Veterans Administration Regional Office, Federal Building, Fort Snelling, St. Paul, Minnesota. File XC-2625-742.
Contains pension and other records of White-Man-Runs-Him.

Dixon, Joseph K. *The Vanishing Race.* New York: Popular Library, 1923.
Contains favorite stories of White-Man-Runs-Him.

Lowie, Robert H. *The Crow Indians.* New York: Rinehart, 1935.
Information on Bull-Chief.

Linderman, Frank B. *Pretty Shield.* Lincoln and London: University of Nebraska, 1932.
Supports the traditional birth of Crow children.

Medicine Crow, Joe. Personal interviews.
16 June 1990. *Buffalo jump on-site inspection.*
19 June 1991. *White-Man-Runs-Him gets his name.*

Mc Allester, David. "Water As A Disciplinary Agent Among The Crow And Blackfoot," *American Anthropologist,* N.S. 43, 1941.
Water as a form of discipline.

Petzoldt, Rev. W. A. "The Life of White-Man-Runs-Him."
Funeral address prepared for the funeral of White-Man-Runs-Him by Rev. Petzoldt.

Plenty Hoops, Winona. Personal Interview.
13 June 1991. On the birth date of White-Man-Runs-Him.

IV. SEEKING STATUS

Like most Crow boys of his time, White-Man-Runs-Him sought to achieve the values of a warrior society in order to gain prestige and political position through the approved structure of that society. He knew that war was considered by his people to be a dangerous yet glorious game, and that if carried out successfully, could lead to status and influence in the tribal community. His father, Bull Chief, had been a successful and honored warrior-chief in his time, and White-Man-Runs-Him desired to achieve similar honors and status when his time came.

There were many chiefs in Crow society. Among them, there was no jealousy, no conflict, no pulling of rank. There was only respect, because each man who attained the title of chief had risked both his life and limb to qualify for the approved war deeds. Only in this way could a young man win the lifelong respect of his fellow tribesmen.

The preparation for actual combat began early in life. White-Man-Runs-Him went on the warpath for the first time at about 13 years old. He did not go as a warrior, but rather as a "water boy" or "holder of the horses." His job, along with several other invited boys, was to help find streams of water and inform the war party where they were located. When the war party discovered the enemy, White-Man-Runs-Him was expected as a holder of horses to do just that. He was not to move until the older warriors returned, often in a hurry, to escape a pursuing enemy. After the return of a successful war party, White-Man-Runs-Him and the other selected youths were asked to guard the great number of Crow horses that sometimes grazed more than twelve miles from the main camp. It was dangerous work for a boy so young.

At about age 14, White-Man-Runs-Him was called upon to aid a war party by moving up to the rank of "helper." Essentially this meant that he was to help set up temporary shelters that were designed to be used on such a journey of combat. The boys who achieved this honor built the fires when it was safe to do so, and in short, provided for the camp in any way the warriors deemed necessary.

Before a young man could take to the warpath himself, he was first expected to participate in a vision quest. On many occasions, White-Man-Runs-Him had heard the tribal crier as he rode through the village appealing to all of the young men and boys who were ready to go to the mountains and fast. The call was probably made in order to qualify more men to fill the depleted war ranks or to simply remind the potential warriors that the time had come for them to take the next step in preparation for full manhood. Along with the other young men, White-Man-Runs-Him had heard the great chiefs talk of medicine, and he had heard the stories of the great feats accomplished by the visionaries of an earlier time. He had also experienced the work and power of the visionaries of his tribe. He had noted the power of medicine in determining the course of battle, and he had witnessed the special healing power of some medicine people.

Before seeking vision, White-Man-Runs-Him went to a Holy Man who prepared him for the ordeal. He understood that at birth every Crow had a sacred helper which he identified only through a dream. If his vision was good, and the sacred helper strong, then he would be protected and live to be an old man, a tribal elder. If the spiritual helper was not powerful, then he might die at a young age on the field of battle.

The Holy Man instructed the young vision seeker that First Worker (Creator) was everywhere and could be found in everything. White-Man-Runs-Him was further told that the first medicine given to the Crow was the sweat which must be taken in preparation for the vision quest. The Holy Man lectured that the steam from the water being poured on the heated rocks was the image of the First Worker. The sweat is sacred and will cleanse not only the body of the initiate but also the soul. He was then told that when he reached his chosen mountain peak, he should pray and weep. "If there was no reason to weep, then he should torture his body and cover the ground with his blood and tears."

When the instruction was complete, White-Man-Runs-Him ventured off into the Big Horn Mountains, above Sheridan, Wyoming. White-Man-Runs-Him told Winona Plenty Hoops that he had to "jump across a tremendous ravine to get to the place where the spirits finally called (named the Big Rocks)." As he had been instructed earlier, he divested himself of all clothing and purified himself in the scent of pine needles to eliminate the human smell. For four days, without food or water, he prayed, wailed, and prepared himself to seek a vision.

If a vision did not come, then he would consider, in the Crow tradition, cutting or chopping off a finger with a knife, or piercing his body, or cutting some flesh from his arms, legs, or chest and sacrificing them to the Creator, with a plea for a blessing.

The first night White-Man-Runs-Him "bedded down" between a grouping of rocks, facing the east. That night a vision came telling him to move to Sheep Mountain, "for the powers would seek him there."

The next day he moved to Sheep Mountain, which to this day is referred to by the Crow as "where White-Man-Runs-Him bedded" or "where he lays down to have visions." Sometime during his sleep, there came to his soul the "Little One that tells things," a good spirit.

Edward Curtis, in his book *The North American Indian*, said that White-Man-Runs-Him "possesses no medicine derived from his

Sheep Mountain, where White-Man-Runs-Him "bedded" to seek vision

own vision." Most Crow did not report to others their vision or medicine until the medicine had been proven in battle or in some personal matter. For other Crow, the sacred power was of such significance that it could not be shared with others. The Crow allowed a tribal member the privilege of purchasing medicine from another member who had special or significant powers. Medicine could be purchased whether or not the buyer had himself experienced a vision.

While White-Man-Runs-Him never totally revealed his vision or the power he received, there is little doubt, however, that his vision quest was successful. For whatever reason that Curtis made reference to the lack of vision by White-Man-Runs-Him, he was wrong. Winona Plenty Hoops said that one of his tepees, still in possession of the family, showed two eagles, one male, and one female. "When the spirits came to him on Sheep Mountain, they walked him around a tepee with two eagles."

The eagles on his tepee may have perpetuated a myth about White-Man-Runs-Him. Wildschut reported in his notes that White-Man-Runs-Him once fasted in the Pryor Mountains at a place called "Where they see the Rope," named in his honor. The peak was so named because the white clay-painted thongs attached to the skewers in his chest were visible to the villagers below. White clay was used in ceremonies to symbolize purity or cleanliness. The story perpetuated by Wildschut proclaims that White-Man-Runs-Him danced around a pole dragging several buffalo skulls tied to rawhide thongs which were attached to the skewers in his body. Each time he went around the pole, lightning flashed. The supernatural flashes, it was said, "could be seen some two hundred miles away by a group of Crow."

As a result of this event, it was said by some that it was here that White-Man-Runs-Him dreamed of seven eagles. One eagle had his eye shut, and each time he opened his eye, lightning flashed. Since one of his tents in later times showed an eagle with its wings wrapped around the tent and lightning coming from the eyes, it was assumed that his power lay with the eagle. Joe Medicine Crow refutes the story saying that White-Man-Runs-Him was not the man who fasted in the Pryor Mountains, and that the seven eagles story is a traditional Crow legend, seven being a sacred number. The Crow believed the eagle

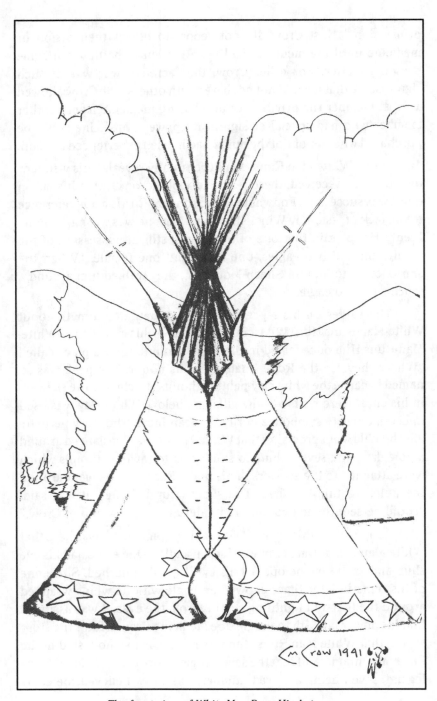

The front view of White-Man-Runs-Him's tepee.

The back view of White-Man-Runs-Him's tepee.

represented the special messenger, who was able to carry prayers to the Everywhere Spirit. It may have been that White-Man-Runs-Him's tepee of eagles reflected the power of the Crow people and his prayer for their success.

While the dream and medicine of White-Man-Runs-Him will probably never be known, a copy of his shield is still possessed by Winona Plenty Hoops. The shield of a warrior most often represented his vision in the miniature. His shield, made from the hide of a buffalo and protected inside a buckskin bag, shows a buffalo facing the west on the front. What it means is uncertain. White-Man-Runs-Him carried his shield on the left arm, and no enemy was allowed to pass to his left.

Dr. Petzoldt relayed on several occasions that White-Man-Runs-Him successfully dreamed with vision and possessed power. Joe Medicine Crow was a witness to White-Man-Runs-Him's possession of

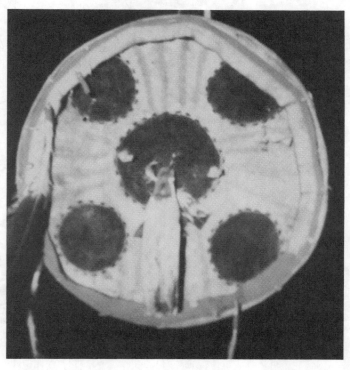

A Crow shield said to be that of White-Man-Runs-Him. Joe Medicine Crow states that the shield is credited to a number of Crow warriors, but is not the shield of White-Man-Runs-Him. The shield is located at the Little Big Horn College, Crow Agency, Montana.

Winona Plenty Hoops with a small replica of White-Man-Runs-Him's shield.

the power. Once when Joe was a boy, he and White-Man-Runs-Him were near Wyola, Montana, when a "tremendous and dangerous hail storm suddenly appeared." When White-Man-Runs-Him saw the storm bearing down on them, "he began to sing his medicine song, and immediately the hail storm moved off course and around us."

When White-Man-Runs-Him came down off Sheep Mountain, his dream successful, he was now considered by warriors to be prepared to accept the challenge of war and to participate in battle. It was in battle where he would have an opportunity to prove to himself and to others his power and individual prowess. Warriors who went out to seek honors were not always successful. Once White-Man-Runs-Him and a group of allies traveled from their camp near Billings over 100 miles to a place near Wyola, where a group of Sioux were supposed to be camped. When they arrived, they found nothing. The return trip, without benefit of honors, must have been a difficult one.

Success on the war trail, however, became very common to White-Man-Runs-Him, and he was known by the Crow, and his enemies as well, as a most successful horse raider. One of the favorite stories still told by his relatives in Montana took place before he enlisted with Gibbon's forces in their move against the Sioux and Cheyenne. On this particular occasion, as the story goes, White-Man-Runs-Him and a group of young men under Red Streak Across His Face (the pipe carrier and leader) went out on foot looking for a Sioux camp. On this day their power was with them, and they discovered a fairly large encampment. As they looked over the camp from a distance, White-Man-Runs-Him noted a prize horse and a mule tethered in front of a lodge. He quickly decided to make the horse his. At just the right moment the warriors started to crawl into the enemy camp. White-Man-Runs-Him noticed several dogs as he neared his objective. He managed to comfort and calm them as he continued to move on toward the horse of his dreams. Upon reaching the horse, he carefully removed the post that was holding the large number of ponies in addition to the one he especially coveted. Quicker than the blink of the eye, the Crow youths jumped on their new found ponies and rode off with all the speed they could attain. They were lucky; they had caught the Sioux by surprise, which would give them a distinct lead in the chase that followed. As the successful war party reached the Little Big Horn River near Wyola, Montana, they decided to stop long enough to water their horses. While the other members of the group stayed on their mounts, White-Man-Runs-Him jumped off his horse to get a drink for himself. Almost as soon as he dismounted, the commander of the group, Red-Streak-Across-His-Face, grabbed White-Man-Runs-Him's new sorrel horse and rode off, leaving the young man confused by the act.

Alone and without a mount, White-Man-Runs-Him hardly had time to think when he observed a Sioux war party coming up fast. Noticing a giant-hollowed out log near the river bank, he decided to crawl in hoping that he would not be discovered by the relatively large group of the enemy. The idea worked, for the Sioux passed on by in their hurried search.

White-Man-Runs-Him crawled out of the log and pondered his next move. As he walked near the river, he looked up and could hardly believe his eyes. The Sioux had given up the chase and were returning by the same route they had taken. White-Man-Runs-Him quickly returned to the log and as before, the Sioux passed by him a second time. Medicine Crow said that the log that housed White-Man-Runs-Him stayed in place for many years and only recently was washed away in high water.

White-Man-Runs-Him considered his options once again, then decided to pursue a very dangerous course of action. It was time to prove himself and his power. He began to run, then walk toward the Sioux camp. At day break, he reached the enemy pony herd, located near the camp. He was almost discovered immediately by a Sioux who seemed to come from nowhere. Luck was with him again. The Sioux shouted to him, "See my horses?" or something to that effect. Because of the similarities of the two languages, White-Man-Runs-Him recognized some of the words. Raising his hands in the air, he shook his head and answered, "No horses." White-Man-Runs-Him decided that he should find a place to hide during the day and crawled under some grapevines near the camp where he lay on his stomach in such a way that he could view the entire area.

Shortly after daybreak an old woman came very near where he was hiding. As she gathered firewood, she stopped momentarily, then hollered something to a man who was moving in the direction of the horse herd. The man laughed and returned some words to the woman who moved off to gather wood elsewhere. Years later, in more peaceful times, White-Man-Runs-Him was talking to some Sioux about mutual experiences. As they conversed, he discovered it was this man's camp he had been in. He also learned that the woman who almost discovered him, had said, "There is a man in those bushes." The man who had laughed had told her not to worry because it was old "what's his name" having sex with someone. The Sioux had remembered that day well, because as night fell, White-Man-Runs-Him crawled out from his grapevine hideout and rode off with between 15 and 30 head of horses.

He decided to drive his newly acquired prizes in a half circle through the Big Horn Mountains. When he arrived at the Crow camp there was a victory celebration in progress. The entire camp was alarmed to see White-Man-Runs-Him with his catch of horses, for they had been told by Red-Streak-Across-His-Face that he was dead. White-Man-Runs-Him's relatives gathered around him to discuss what had happened. When they learned what had happened, they immediately went to Red-Streak, challenging him to return the sorrel horse that belonged to their relative. Red-Streak returned the horse and was forever disgraced in the minds of the Crow. He would leave the tribe sometime later to live in the mountains by himself. White-Man-Runs-Him had proven his power.

According to the Crow structure, his successful experience qualified him to become a scout. A scout was charged with finding the safe way, noticing the signs, finding the proper camping grounds, and being the eyes and ears of his fellow warriors in their search for an enemy. If he proved to be good enough, then he might be recognized as Chief of Scouts, which would allow him to be placed in a leadership position on the campaign.

If a Crow warrior had completed just one successful war deed, he was referred to as a "Good Man," for he risked his life in battle. He would now be entitled to lead. Success in leading others permitted him to be a campaign planner, to be in charge of others. He was deemed to be a leader, not an ordinary man, but a pipe carrier, who had proven powers and exceptional status.

If a man had accomplished all of these things, and had met the four war deed requirements, then he became a full-fledged chief. The successful chief must capture a horse from the enemy camp by "cutting the rope," which meant entering the enemy camp, passing their warning systems, including the dogs, and cutting the rope tied around the enemy's horse – which was sometimes attached to the owner's hand inside the tepee.

He was also expected to capture an enemy's weapon by wrestling it away from him in any manner possible. A third requirement necessary to reach full chieftainship included counting coup by striking an enemy with a coup stick, quirt, or a bow. The fourth war deed could be granted only upon the return of a successful war party led by the potential chief. This meant that the war party should return with the spoils of war and without the loss of life. If a life had been taken by the enemy the war deed was not given. It was also expected that if a returning war party was pursued by the enemy, the leader would go far to the rear, behind his men and in front of the enemy, until the party had moved safely away.

In each case, the warrior who was successful in accomplishing a war deed was publicly given his deed by the Council of Chiefs, and when possible, supported by witnesses and the leaders of the war party. The warrior was praised and led throughout the village as he recounted his deed to all. He was esteemed by his clansmen, songs were made up and sung in his behalf, and a dance was held in his honor. The celebrations of honor sometimes lasted throughout the night into the next day.

The marks or symbols of those who had successfully completed war deeds were obvious to others and further raised the status of the warrior. An eagle feather in the hair signified the counting of coup, as did wolf tails attached to the heels of the moccasins. A warrior who had taken a weapon from the enemy could decorate his shirt with ermine or even scalps.

For his efforts on the horse raid, White-Man-Runs-Him was given two war deeds by the Council of Chiefs. He had not only been successful twice in raiding an enemy camp, but he was given credit for leading a war party when he single handedly returned to the Sioux camp and brought home a herd of horses. It was something special to bring home so many horses. The Crow were the richest nation east of the Rocky Mountains, with the average family possessing 100 head or so of horses. The Crow valued horses as much or more than any other tribe. White-Man-Runs-Him dressed himself in ermine and his brethren took notice.

The status of White-Man-Runs-Him was further enhanced when he was recruited to join one of the warrior fraternities, open only to those who had accomplished battle. While there had been more warrior lodges in earlier times, the main fraternities in the 1860s and 1870s were the Lumpwoods, Foxes, Big Dogs, Muddy Hands, and the Ravens. The Foxes and Lumpwoods were the largest and most influential lodges.

Each fraternity recruited young men, chose their own leaders, set up their own rules and customs, and developed their own standards to demonstrate membership and status. The various societies competed against each other, both as individuals and as groups. Parades were held, songs sung, and members of the opposing groups were teased and humiliated for having lost a contest on the field of battle or in a friendly competition.

The Lumpwoods, were successful in recruiting White-Man-Runs-Him. The Lumpwoods was the largest and most popular military lodge of this time period, traditionally giving presents to help recruit new members. Generally, the chief designated one of the societies to police and control the hunt, move the camp, and carry out other duties necessary to tribal life and survival. If a member of the Lumpwoods was killed in combat, then his group presented gifts to a close relative of the deceased. The name Lumpwoods, legend says, came from the use of a knobbed stick by a warrior of long ago.

An interesting sidelight in the relationship and competitions between the Lumpwoods and Foxes was that after the election of officers in the spring of the year, a Lumpwoods or Fox member was entitled to kidnap a woman of the opposite society, provided he had been intimate with her prior to her marriage. When the time came to capture the woman, the husband had to let her go showing no emotion. If he resisted the theft, he lost status, was ridiculed, had songs made up about him designed to humiliate, and his property was destroyed. If he tried to reclaim his wife or remarry her later, he was tied up and dog excrement rubbed on him.

White-Man-Runs-Him was proud to be a Lumpwood. His honors had been noticed. By Crow standards he was now a chief. He was not yet 18 years of age, but would he be able to fulfill the other two deeds necessary to become a full chief? Would he have the chance, or would his life and the times change so fast that he would have little opportunity to fulfill his desired goals? He was well aware that to be the chief of all, his war deeds would have to be so numerous that the Council of Chiefs, along with his military lodge, and the Crow people, would willingly give their consent to his status.

To become involved in tribal politics and leadership, a warrior must first prove himself as a warrior. Then as a warrior society chief, together with other chiefs, elders, and holy men, he could make decisions for the band or the tribe. To become a band chief was not easy. Not only did the war deeds have to be accomplished, but the man must have great wisdom in human affairs in order to maintain tribal unity and harmony. He must have an upright character and a good personality, always being honest, fair, and kind. He must be benevolent to all his people and see to it that all were provided with the necessities of life. His house must be open to the poor so that they could find food. If those who needed help did not come to the house of the chief, he must invite them. In addition, a good chief was never to ask help of others.

When men came in the evening to converse and exchange views, White-Man-Runs-Him noticed that the chief instructed the crier to welcome all, for "food and tobacco is prepared for you." A chief also had to have good and strong medicine or the spiritual insight to cope with unusual and supernatural situations.

The chief of the Crow truly had to be a special person. He was granted his position by his people. He had built up a following based upon his war exploits and his proven ability to fulfill Crow ideals and values of leadership. Only by continuing to excel could a chief maintain the faith of the people and thus remain in that position.

White-Man-Runs-Him in full dress. (Courtesy of the Montana State Historical Society)

SOURCES

Chapter IV

Curtis, Edward S. *The North American Indian.* Vol. III. New York: Johnson Reprint Corporation, 1908.
Claims White-Man-Runs-Him had no vision experience.

Lowie, Robert. "The Religion of the Crow." *Anthropological Paper American Museum of Natural History.* Vol. XXV., 1922.
Visions.

Lowie, Robert. "Social Life of the Crow Indians." *Anthropological Paper American Museum of Natural History,* Vol. IX.
War customs.

Lowie, Robert. "Societies of the Crow Hidatsa and Mandan Indians," *Anthropological Paper American Museum of Natural History,* Vol. XI.,
Military lodges and Fraternities.

Lowie, Robert. *The Crow Indians.* Lincoln and London: University of Nebraska Press, 1935.
War honors and deeds.

Medicine Crow, Joe. *"The Making of a Crow Chief."* Big Woods/Big Plains Lecture Series. Stillwater, Minnesota, 9 April 1988.
The process and personality needed to become a full chief.

Medicine Crow, Joe. *"White-Man-Runs-Him."* Big Woods/Big Plains Lecture Series. Stillwater, Minnesota, 10 April 1990.
Stories of White-Man-Runs-Him including war honors.

Nabokov, Peter. *Two Leggings.* Lincoln and London: University of Nebraska Press, 1967.
Contains William Wildschut's description of where White-Man-Runs-Him fasted.

Petzoldt, Rev. W. A. "The Life of White-Man-Runs-Him." Funeral address prepared for the funeral of White-Man-Runs-Him by Petzoldt. The speech was provided by Robert Lix, Post Adjutant, White-Man-Runs-Him Post No. 16, Lodge Grass, Montana.

Plenty Hoops, Winona. Personal interview.
13 June 1991. *White-Man-Runs-Him's vision quest.*

V. THE SIOUX ARE FORCED WEST

After the great migration from the east coast, and their separation from other bands, the Siouan people, as we know them today,
lived for many years in Minnesota, Wisconsin, Michigan , Iowa, and
the Dakotas. They came to believe that their nation had its birth at
Mille Lacs Lake in northern Minnesota. Even before the first white
men found the Sioux living near and around the lakes of Minnesota
and Wisconsin, two of the three major Siouan groups had already left
for the plains. The Teton left first, followed by the Yanktons. They left
because their numbers were growing and it became apparent that new
food sources would be needed soon. The third major Siouan group,
the Santee, remained in the Mille Lacs Lake area until the Chippewa
came with their new trade guns, driving the Santee south, where they
settled in scattered villages along the Mississippi River from St. Paul
to Winona, Minnesota. No matter where the various bands traveled
throughout their territory of Minnesota, Wisconsin, Iowa, and North
and South Dakota, they continued to trade, communicate, and
maintain their kinship relations and traditions.

The western Sioux noted with interest that Zebulon Pike,
representing the U.S. government, traded the Santee $200 worth of
trade goods for two pieces of land to be used for the building of forts.
The original treaty called for the Santee to get $2,000 for the land at
the junction of the Minnesota and Mississippi, upon which Fort
Snelling would be built, and at the mouth of the St. Croix River, which
would never be used for the building of a fort. The Santee never saw
the $2,000. The trade goods were all they got.

Along with the white traders and farmers that came to the land
of the Santee came disease, whiskey, missionaries, schools, and of
course, the desire for Indian land. In the Treaty of Traverse des Sioux,
1851, the Santee gave up their claims to lands in Minnesota, Iowa, and
the Dakotas for a reservation 10 miles on either side of the Minnesota
River, from the Yellow Medicine Tributary to Lake Traverse. For the

MINNESOTA

cession of land, they were to receive $1,410,000. Some of the money was to remain in trust with the remaining portions used to move the Santee to their new home, pay supposed trade debts to dishonest traders, and cover reservation development. The Santee had sold their land for 12½ cents per acre.

The white advance came to Minnesota so fast that the traditional hunting grounds were taken before the Santee could adjust to a different lifestyle. Many young men seeking traditional goals were frustrated by the broken promises and the seemingly hopeless life of becoming farmers. The volatile atmosphere was further strengthened when Inkpaduta and his band carried out what is referred to as the

"Spirit Lake Massacre" in Iowa, killing 40 people. Even though the Santee were told to go after Inkpaduta and bring him in or face loss of annuity payments, Inkpaduta was never caught. He and his sons joined forces with the Sioux on the plains, and Inkpaduta led a Santee contingent at the battle of the Little Big Horn. Ventures such as those of Inkpaduta encouraged the more militant young men to believe they could succeed in war with the whites.

In 1858, the Santee were again called upon to give up their rich land on the north side of the Minnesota River in order to gain funds needed for their survival. The Santee were to get $260,000, but much of the money went to traders for debts they said were owed them by the Sioux. Many unhappy traditional warriors began to attack farm animals in the Minnesota River Valley.

The winter of 1861-62 was unusually cold, and many Santee families faced starvation. The summer brought no relief. Crops failed, little food was available at the agencies, and they were told that annuities would be delayed for several months due to the Civil War. Problems were further increased when a group of warriors demanded credit from the traders at the trading posts. One trader, Andrew Myrick, told them there would be no credit, and as far as he was concerned they could "eat grass or their own dung."

An incident in Meeker County sparked the Minnesota-Dakota conflict. Several hungry hunters returning from an unsuccessful hunt found some chicken eggs in a ditch. One of the hunters told the others not to eat the eggs because they belonged to a white man. They argued, questioned each other's courage, then went to the house where they engaged the owner, Mr. Jones, in conversation. For whatever reasons, the party, along with Mr. Jones, began walking to a neighbor's home. When they got to the Baker residence, the Indians challenged the whites to a shooting contest. At some point the Indians turned their guns on the whites, killing four people. The warriors stole two horses and headed back to the reservation where they called together the warriors lodge to tell what they had done. Discussing all of the abuses of the whites, including the fact that most soldiers had left Minnesota for the Civil War, the confidence of the traditional Sioux grew to the point where they believed they must go to war.

Little Crow, leader of the Dakota-Minnesota Conflict of 1862. (Courtesy of the Smithsonian Institute)

Initially Little Crow, the chosen war leader, counseled the warrior groups not to fight:

> You are full of white man's devil water. You are like dogs in the Hot Moon when they run and snap at their own shadows. We are only little herds of buffalo left scattered, but the white men are like the locusts when they fly so thick that the whole sky is a snow storm. You may kill one — two — ten — yes, as many as the leaves in the forest yonder, and their brothers will not miss them. Do you hear the thunder of their big guns. No, it would take you two moons to run down to where they are fighting, and all the way your path would be among white soldiers. You will die like the rabbits when the hungry wolves hunt them in the hard moon. Ta-oh-ya-te-duta is not a coward. He will die with you.

The pressure was too great and the problems too many. Little Crow led the Dakota throughout the Minnesota Valley killing at least 800 and maybe as many as 1,000 people before they faced defeat at the hands of Henry Sibley. Little Crow fled to the west and to Canada where he sought alliances with other nations, including the Ojibway and the British. His diplomacy was of no avail, so he decided to return to Minnesota to steal some horses and then take his family and small following to the plains, where he would join his cousins, hunt the buffalo, and live in peace or war, whatever fate might bring.

Meanwhile, of the 2,200 Santee who surrendered to Sibley, 303 were condemned to death for their participation in the conflict. President Lincoln himself reduced the number to 38, who were hung in Mankato, December 26, 1862. This was the largest mass execution in American history. The Sioux will never forget the bravery shown by the condemned as they painted their bodies and marched to the gallows singing their death songs. Three-hundred twenty-six Santee were sent to a prison in Davenport, Iowa where over one third died before their three-year term was up. The families and dependents of the prisoners interned at Fort Snelling faced ridicule and attack by the white citizens of the area until they were finally removed to the Crow Creek Reservation on the Upper Missouri. From there they were moved to Santee, Nebraska. Many died in the process of removal or from the depressing conditions of the reservations.

Little Crow, the leader of the Santee, was killed while picking berries near Hutchinson, Minnesota, July 3, 1863, by Nathan Lampson and his son Chauncey. Shot first in the groin, Little Crow wounded the elder Lampson in the shoulder, but was finally shot in the chest by Chauncey. Chauncey ran for help as Wowinape, Little Crow's son, went a number of times to a nearby pond for water for his father before he died. Wowinape then dressed his father in new moccasins, folded his arms, wrapped him in a blanket, took his medicine bundle, and fled the area.

When Chauncey returned with help for Nathan, Little Crow was scalped and his body taken to Hutchinson, where he was identified by two deformed wrists which had been shattered by a rifle ball in an earlier dispute with his brothers over the tribal chieftainship. A rope was put around his body, and he was dragged through Hutchinson. Young boys put firecrackers in his ears, mouth, and nose. When some citizens protested, he was buried under a few inches of soil. Then a military officer dug up the body with his sword and beheaded him. A rail was driven into his head and it was paraded through the town. Finally, a Dr. Twichell took the trunk, dismembered it, and lowered it into steam to allow the flesh to disintegrate. A wash-boiler was then used to boil the flesh off the skull. The skull was later presented to the Minnesota State Historical Society, where it was placed on display in the Capitol and later in the Historical Society building in St. Paul. Nathan Lampson received $500 for killing Little Crow, and his son received $75 from the state of Minnesota for the scalp. The Sioux of the plains would not forget the Minnesota experience and the horrific treatment of Little Crow.

At least 800 Santee fled to the west to join their Siouan relatives. It was the military's view that the Sioux would return to Minnesota during the summer to carry on the attacks. Therefore, the decision was made to instead bring the battle to the Indians on the plains. Henry Sibley left Redwood Falls in June, 1863, and engaged the Sioux in battles at Big Mound, North Dakota on June 20, and at Dead Buffalo Lake, North Dakota on June 26, without significant consequences.

General Sully, with a band of cavalry, moved up the Missouri from Fort Randall, in southeastern South Dakota, and met the Sioux in battle in August at Whitestone Hill, North Dakota, destroying their property, capturing a few prisoners, but with little effect other than dispersing the bands. Sully returned with an expedition in 1864, and with a combined force of 2,200 men, including the forces of the Eighth Minnesota under Colonel Minor Thomas, met a big village of Sioux at Killdeer Mountain, southeast of present day Watford City, North Dakota. After fighting all day on July 28, the Sioux gathered together their women and children and fled the field with perhaps as many as 100 dead. Sully reported five dead and 10 wounded. He returned in 1865, but found no Sioux to engage. Thus the conflict moved from the "Big Woods" of Minnesota to the "Big Plains."

After the Minnesota-Dakota Conflict of 1862, events began to move quickly in the land to the west. Gold was discovered in Montana at Gold Creek in 1858, and at Bannack and Alder Gulch in 1862. John Bozeman blazed a trail to the gold fields and the rush into Montana was on; gold was discovered in Helena in 1864 and the Montana Territory was created in the same year. By 1865, Virginia City had been named the territorial capitol.

On November 29, 1864, Reverend Chivington, a Colonel in the Colorado 2nd, attacked Black Kettle's camp, which was flying both an American and a white flag. His men took over 100 Cheyenne scalps, and committed unbelievable perverse acts during the course of battle. A number of men displayed human body parts on their saddles and persons. The angry Southern Cheyenne moved to the Powder River country in the north where they presented the Pipe of Peace to the Sioux and their Northern Cheyenne relatives. Almost as soon as the alliance was consummated, attacks on whites increased.

The Wyoming territory had been created in 1865, and with the conclusion of the Civil War, more immigrants appeared in their wagons. Red Cloud began to rally the Sioux arguing that the "noisy whites" were disrupting the buffalo herds and causing them and other game to leave the area. Red Cloud was especially concerned when the army began to construct Fort Phil Kearney along the Piney Creek, a branch of the Powder River, and found out that Fort C. F. Smith was to be built some 90 miles north. The purpose of the forts was to protect travelers along the Bozeman Trail, which started on the North Platte and moved northwest, cutting across the Powder, Tongue, and Bighorn Rivers, then on to the upper Yellowstone and Virginia City and other mining camps. To Red Cloud and the Sioux, the forts and roads were proof that the whites were "eating up the Indian's" land. This meant war.

Fort Phil Kearney was completed on July 15, 1866. Within 48 hours of its completion, the complex was attacked. Cattle were driven off, wood trains attacked, and the fort was under a general siege for almost two years. From August 1 to December 31, 1866, 154 were killed and 20 wounded. Included in the dead were 81 officers and men who, under Captain William Fetterman, rode out of the fort on December 21, 1866, to relieve the wood train and were attacked by the Sioux and all killed. Fetterman had once boasted that he "could ride through the entire Sioux nation with 80 men." Now he and all his men were dead, scalped, stripped of their clothing, mutilated, with many of them having their penises placed in their mouths, a symbol of great humiliation.

Even though the soldiers were somewhat successful in the Wagon Box and Hayfield battles that followed, the constant warfare with the Sioux and Cheyenne caused the government to reason that if peace could be established, the Union Pacific Railroad could be built with branch lines into the gold fields of Montana, thus avoiding the Indian forces. They believed that time itself would ultimately take care of the Indians as civilization advanced into the area.

When the commissioners met with Red Cloud, they quickly realized that his only real concern was to protect the hunting ground of the Powder River area. If the soldiers would withdraw from the forts, the Sioux would cease fighting.

While the resulting Treaty of 1868 looked very much like Washington had admitted defeat to the Sioux and Cheyenne, it was the goal of the government to place the Sioux on a defined reservation so it would be easier in the future to control them. Hostilities ended between the two parties and anyone on either side who broke the agreement was to be punished. The treaty set up a permanent reservation that was to include all of South Dakota west of the Missouri River. The United States conceded the forts in the Powder River area and the Bozeman Trail while creating "unceded land," free of whites, from the Great Sioux Reservation to the Big Horn Mountains. The treaty also called for a census to be taken and the establishment of schools for the education of Indian children. The

Sioux agreed to withdraw opposition to the Union Pacific Railroad and to permit the construction of any other railroads not passing over their reservation.

For the Crow, the Treaty of 1868 meant that their original land claim had been reduced to 9 million acres. They were promised a new agency that was established by Brigadier General Alfred Sully, Superintendent of Indian Affairs, Montana, on the west bank of Mission Creek, about nine miles northeast of Livingston, Montana. They were also given a doctor, and help in selecting the proper land for farming. Each Crow family was to be given supplies if the head man worked. Both the United States and the Crow agreed that in any future agreements between them, only a majority of Crow males could cede additional land.

Meanwhile, many Sioux leaders like Crazy Horse, Sitting Bull, Gall, and Black Moon refused to sign the treaty of 1868, or to settle on the reservation. Instead they continued to roam and live in the traditional way, encouraging the reservation or "Agency" people to leave. Many Sioux left their agencies to hunt, then returned to the reservation for the winter months. It was the hope of the government that the destruction of the buffalo would eventually bring in those Sioux who refused reservation life.

Financed by Jay Cooke, the Northern Pacific Railroad was chartered in 1864 to complete a route from Lake Superior to Portland, Oregon. While the Treaty of 1868 appeared to prohibit the construction of railroads through Indian territory, a certain clause inserted by the commissioners allowed railways to be built across the reservation if ordered by laws of the United States. It is doubtful if this was read to the Sioux or explained to them. They may have been so happy to get rid of the forts that this issue was of no concern to them. In 1871, surveyors for the Northern Pacific entered the Sioux reservation without permission, and as far as the Sioux were concerned, were in violation of the Treaty of 1868. Lt. Colonel George Armstrong Custer was assigned to the "Yellowstone expedition," to protect surveying parties from the Indian raids that began under the direction of Sitting Bull and other militant leaders. In 1874, Custer's Black Hills expedition confirmed the claim of prospectors that there was gold in the Black Hills.

Custer, the so-called hero of the Washita, where his troops had attacked and killed the peace-minded Black Kettle and dispersed his camp in a winter campaign in November, 1868, had also entered the Black Hills without permission of the Sioux. Now, the gold rush was on. While the government initially tried to prevent the entry of prospectors into the hills, they soon gave up, finding it impossible. However, they did send in a peace commission in an attempt to purchase the rights to mine the gold in the hills. The Commission of 1875 returned to Washington after failing to convince the Sioux with an unrealistic monetary offer.

In the winter of 1875, the Sioux came to realize that the white man would never leave them alone. Runners were sent out in December to every roaming Sioux camp instructing them to come in to the reservations. The winter of 1875 was a particularly hard winter and to move the camps would be disastrous for the welfare of tribal members. When Sitting Bull heard about General Alfred Terry's January 1, 1876, deadline, he laughed and said, "Come and get me, you won't need guides, I won't run away." The traditional Sioux had no intention of coming in and the reservation people were beginning to believe it was time to defend what was left of the land.

SOURCES

Chapter V

Anderson, Gary Clayton. *Little Crow, Spokesman For The Sioux*. St. Paul: Historical Society Press, 1986.
Little Crow and The Dakota-White Conflict of 1862.

Anderson, Gary Clayton and Alan R. Woolworth (ed.) *Through Dakota Eyes*. St. Paul: Minnesota Historical Society Press, 1988.
The Minnesota-Dakota Conflict of 1862 as the Dakota viewed it.

Benjamin, Dr. John and W. W. Pendergast. "Little Crow, The Sioux Chief." *St. Paul Pioneer Press,* July 10, 1863.
His death.

Carley, Kenneth. *The Sioux Uprising of 1862*. St. Paul: The Minnesota Historical Society Press, 1976.
The Dakota Conflict.

Folwell, William Watts. *A History of Minnesota, Vol. II*. St. Paul: Minnesota Historical Society Press, 1924.

Hyde, George. *Red Cloud's Folk*. Nornam: University of Oklahoma Press, 1967.

Meyer, Roy. *History of the Santee Sioux*. Lincoln: University of Nebraska, 1967.

Robinson, Doane. *A History of the Dakota or Sioux Indians*. Minneapolis: Reprint, Ross and Haines, 1967.

Sneve, Virginia Driving Hawk. *They Led A Nation*. Sioux Falls: Brevet Press, Inc., 1975.
Leaders of the Sioux.

VI. THE ENLISTMENT

When the Sioux did not comply with the government's directive, it was the Secretary of the Interior, on February 1, 1876, who declared all Indians in the unceded territory of 1868 as "hostile." General Sheridan looked upon the edict as an opportunity to catch the Sioux sleeping, when their horses were weak from the winter and needed the feed of the spring to revive for war. Sheridan's plan called for Crook to lead one of the units from Fort Fetterman, Wyoming, on the North Platte. A second force under General Terry was to leave from Fort Lincoln, North Dakota, while the third unit was to move out from Fort Shaw, Montana, under Col. John Gibbon. No plan of specific action was commanded, as it was believed that each and any unit could meet and defeat any of the so-called "hostiles" they might find.

Crook, with a force of 800 cavalry and infantry, was the first to march on the Sioux. On March 17, he discovered a village. Sending Col. Reynolds with six companies of cavalry, he attacked a camp on the Powder River. The surprised and confused Sioux scattered, then rallied to defeat the cautious Reynolds. Crook, upset with Reynolds, returned to Fort Fetterman to heal the wounded and prepare for another campaign two months later.

Meanwhile, Col. Gibbon left Fort Ellis with 450 men of the Second Cavalry and Seventh Infantry. Gibbon's objective was to keep the enemy south of the Yellowstone, thus preventing the Sioux and their allies from entering the north sections of the Yellowstone Valley. With Crook in pursuit of the assumed small number of Sioux, Gibbon was to move to the Rosebud as soon as possible. It was feared that because of the high April water, the Indians might get across the Rosebud, either above or below the mouth, which was their normal crossing point during high water times.

With Gibbon's infantry camped above the mouth of the Stillwater River, and his cavalry near the ford in the stream several miles upstream, he sent word to the Crow Agency that he wanted to meet

73

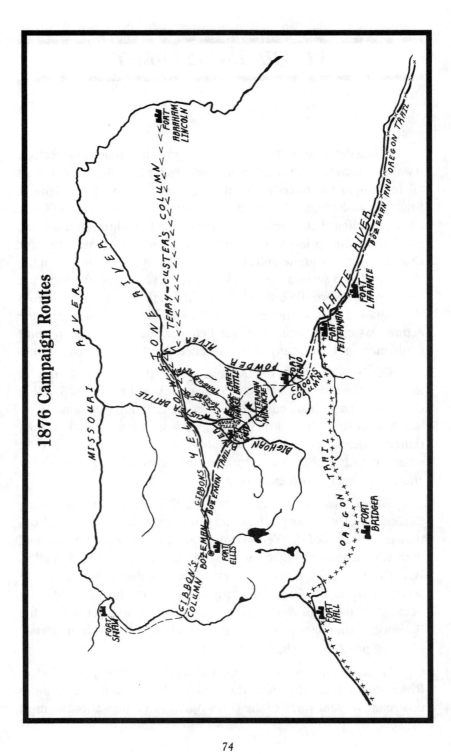

1876 Campaign Routes

with them for the purpose of enlisting scouts. Gibbon had hired a half-blood Sioux, Mitch Bouyer, who spoke English, Sioux, and Crow, to guide his contingent of soldiers. Bouyer contacted the Crow and reported back that they were ready to hold council with him. The attitude of the Crow was less than enthusiastic, but since they were already coming into the agency to claim their annuity payments, they decided they might just as well meet with the soldiers.

Gibbon's advance group was commanded by Lt. Bradley and they arrived at the Crow Agency near Livingston on April 9. He brought with him 25 men from Company E. Gibbon was to arrive with several other officers later the same day. It was Bradley's job to record the talks. A man called Pierre Chien acted as the interpreter, with Thomas Leforge and Tom Stewart being given the responsibility of reviewing and checking the dialogue to make sure the correct interpretations were achieved.

When the leaders of the Crow had gathered together, the council began. The two principle chiefs and spokesmen for the Crow were Sits-in-the-Middle-of-the-Land, or Blackfoot, as the whites called him, and Iron Bull. It was Sits-in-the-Middle-of-the-Land who had signed the Treaty of 1868 and now noted that "it had not done much good" in terms of preventing the Sioux from violating Crow lands. He warned Bradley before the council began that the Sioux were coming and that he could not afford to let his warriors go. Bradley countered that the Crow had signed a treaty in 1825 which implied that they would help the whites when they were in trouble. Sits-in-the Middle-of-the-Land then said, "I understand, but I will never order my men to go."

As the discussions of the council proceeded, Sits-in-the-Middle-of-the-Land expressed his concern that should the Crow go along as scouts, the army might mistake them for Sioux and shoot them. As the discussions continued, it was apparent to the army officials the Crow were generally reluctant, but they agreed to discuss the scouting offer further among themselves. Then Gibbon rose to speak:

> I have come down here to make war on the Sioux. The Sioux are your enemy and ours. For a long while they have been killing white men and killing Crow. I am going down to punish the Sioux for making war upon the white man. If the Crow want to make war upon

the Sioux, now is their time. If they want to drive them from their country and prevent them from sending war parties into their country to murder their men, now is the time. If they want to get revenge for Crows that have fallen, to get revenge for the killing of such men as the Gallant Soldier, Long Horse, now is their time.

The Crow discussed what Gibbon had said among themselves. Finally, Sits-in-the-Middle-of-the-Land stood and expressed his concern that the Sioux might come while the men were away with the army. He further wondered how long the men would be gone. His questions were not answered as Gibbon spoke again, portraying tremendous confidence and predicting the defeat of the Sioux by the great number of soldiers who were to be gathered. He told those assembled that some day the Crow would be proud of their participation with the whites in the defeat of their enemy, the Sioux.

According to White-Man-Runs-Him, by this time the Crow were somewhat "wary of the white man and his promises." Some of the discussion had attempted to focus on the fact that the government had not fulfilled its rationing commitment. Gibbon tried to explain he did not have the authority to resolve any of the Crow problems, and they would have to work out such treaty problems with their agent. Turning back to the question of scouting, Gibbon spoke again:

> White men and red men make war in a different way. The white man goes through the country with his head down and sees nothing. The red man keeps his eyes open and can see better than a white man. Now, I want some young warriors of the Crow to go along with me, who will use their eyes and tell me what they see. I don't want men who are willing to ride along with my men and stay with the wagon, I have plenty of those. I want young, active, brave men, who will be my eyes. I want 25 such men; men who will find out where the Sioux are so that I can go after them. They will be soldiers of the government, get soldier's pay and soldier's food, and, when I come back they will come back with me and join their tribe again.

Old Crow cautioned Gibbon to slow down because his people needed to talk further. White Mouth then accused the whites of taking the Crow on expeditions before and doing nothing to help them afterwards. Mountain Pocket added, "I have fought the Sioux till I am tired. You want to fight now — I'll let you go alone."

Sits-in-the-Middle-of-the-Land ("Blackfoot") and his wife at Fort Laramie, 1868. (Picture courtesy of Mr. and Mrs. George Cooley, Sheridan, WY)

Old Crow spoke once again:

I am a warrior, I led a party, I went to war, I found a camp, I told the young men to charge. I have done so many times. I always do what I set out to do. If you go and find the Sioux and don't want to fight and tie the young men down, they would cry and break loose and go straight to the battle and get killed and that would be bad. You had better go alone.

Gibbon responded:

There is always danger in going to war. Men usually go to war thinking that they may be killed. Men who want to sleep in their tepees every night don't want to go to war. We don't go that way, we don't want anybody who goes to war that way.

I have heard several of you talk, the talk all seems to be one way. Now I want to hear from the other side. If any of you want to go to war, I want to hear from you. If not, there is an end of it.

Iron Bull now stood up, walked over to Gibbon, shook his hand, and said, "I want to know what route you are going to take." Gibbon answered, "I am going after Indians —never mind which route." Iron Bull then stated:

When this agency was established, there were in succession several agents for the Crows. We begged them all to take pity on us and help us fight the Sioux. They would not, so we went and fought them alone, though there were not many of us. You say the Sioux are your enemies; so, too, they are mine. You tell us that you are hunting the Sioux, that you have your way of doing it; so, too, have we our way of going to war. If our young men seek the Sioux, they travel night and day till they find them; then they do what they went to do and return. In any other way nothing could be done. You have not told us how long you are going to be gone. If our young men go with you, you will put white men's clothes on them.

Gibbon answered, "I shall only give them a strip of red." Old Crow got back in the discussion:

If you take some of the Crows along with you and you find a camp of Sioux and have a fight, I would like to have you send our young men back to see us afterwards. We see each other —we are here together. You tell me what you want with me; I will now tell you what I want with you. If the Crows go with you, and they find a camp, they will bark like a dog. Will you then jump on the camp and fight right there?

Gibbon agreed, by saying, "That is what we want." Old Crow seemed encouraged as he stated: "That is good. Be patient, do not hurry us. You have told us what you want; now let us hold a council among ourselves and see who will go with you and who will not." Gibbon said, "I am waiting; I will be here two days." Old Crow replied to Gibbon:

> That will be enough. The Sioux are a very strong people, a very brave people. Our scouts report to the chief where the camp is, and tell him to get up and go to the camp. Will you believe what the young men tell you? When we go to war, we generally send out a scouting party. If they find a camp, they bark like a wolf.

When Gibbon withdrew from the discussion he was very concerned about the ultimate outcome. It was apparent to Gibbon that the two leaders, Sits-in-the-Middle-of-the-Land and Iron Bull, could speak only for themselves. Each warrior would ultimately make his own decision.

White-Man-Runs-Him had made up his mind even before the council began. He recalled that his thoughts were of the "vision of Spotted Horse of many years ago which told them to be friends with and help the white man."

He remembered the words of an ancient wise man: "We will marry our women to the whites. We have always had to take care of the few that have come this way. Our blood will be theirs and their blood in ours. When they take our land and buffalo they will treat us kindly because they are one with us." He considered the dreams of his contemporary, Medicine Crow, whose visions in his youth included seeing something black, with round legs, puffing smoke and pulling boxlike objects behind it, coming down the Valley of Chieftains of the Little Big Horn River [30 years later, the Big Horn Southern Railroad became a fact].

Another vision saw a white man coming from the east, saying, "I come from the land of the rising sun, where many, many white men live. They are coming and will, in time, take possession of your land. At that time, you will be a great chief of your tribe. Do not oppose these but deal with them wisely and all will turn out all right." In still another vision he foresaw the Crow country covered with large herds of "horse buffalo" or cattle [Medicine Crow died before his vision of "wagons traveling in the air" came to pass].

White-Man-Runs-Him was also well aware of the visions of Plenty Coups, who along with Medicine Crow, is considered the last of the traditional chiefs. Plenty Coups dreamed that in his lifetime the buffalo would disappear and they would be replaced by bulls, cows, and calves of the whites. He dreamed the whites would take control of the Crow country and their cattle would cover the plains. In his dream Plenty Coups was instructed to "think for himself, to listen, to learn to avoid disaster by the experiences of others."

He interpreted his dream as a warning. Those tribes that had fought the white man had been defeated. By listening to the "dream bird," the Crow could still escape and keep their lands. The dream featured a forest of trees said to represent the great nations. Then came four winds that left only one nation still in place, the nation of the Crow, which had never warred with the white man. In a sense, the dream became a direction for the Crow, a direction based upon the visions and experiences of others who had lived a long time ago.

Years after the Battle of the Little Big Horn, White-Man-Runs-Him told Dixon:

> The Great Father at Washington sent representatives out to our country. The Indians met them and held a council. The Sioux were the hereditary enemies of the Crow. The head man sent by the Great Father said to the Crow. We must get together and fight and get this land from the Sioux. We must win it by conquest. We loved our land so we consented to go in with the soldiers and put these other tribes off the land. The soldiers and I were fighting in friendship; what they said, I did and what I said, they did. So I helped my tribe. Land is a very valuable thing and especially our land. I knew the Cheyennes and Sioux wanted to take it by conquest, so I stayed with the soldiers to help hold it.

Many young Crow were prepared to go against the Sioux for a variety of individual reasons. In addition to the reasons he gave Dixon, White-Man-Runs-Him viewed joining with Gibbon's forces as a fulfillment of his cultural objective: that of gaining additional war honors.

He was especially happy when Sits-in-the-Middle-of-the-Land rose at the Council meeting the next day and said, "Take care of my men." The enlistment of Crow was underway. White-Man-Runs-Him was one of the first to sign up on April 10, 1876. His military records indicate that he signed up until he was to be discharged, which usually meant a six-month tour of duty.

Gibbon had hoped to enlist 25 scouts. He was able to sign up 23 Crow and two whites who were living with the Crow at the time. Tom LeForge and Barney Bravo were hired as interpreters and as scouts. LeForge stated in *Memoirs of a White Crow Indian* that Lt. Bradley told him, "In addition to the small army allowance for scouting, he would pay him one dollar per day for special service to him as a monitor of the lore of the country, the geography of it, and the ways of the Indians."

The ages of the Crow scouts who signed on ranged from 16 to 60. It was the belief of White-Man-Runs-Him that the older men were enlisted to help "advise and control the more youthful scouts" who would have to do the bulk of the hard scouting.

The Bradley Diary states:

> The scouts were sworn in on the point of a knife which was pressed to their index finger. The scouts then requested that Gibbon take the same oath, promising to believe their reports and doing what the scouts wanted him to do. Gibbon tried to have it explained to the scouts that it was they who must do as ordered and in this relationship it was a one-sided obligation.

Gibbon placed Bradley in command of the scouts on the morning of April 10. After informing the scouts that their pay, rations, and allowances would be the same as the enlisted men, Bradley took the Crow oath himself and touched the point of the knife with his finger in the accepted manner. White-Man-Runs-Him and the other scouts were given an identification badge which consisted of a red piece of cloth that was to be worn on the left arm above the elbow. They were then informed their pay would be $16 per month, with an additional $12 per month being given for their horses. They would be paid every two months.

White-Man-Runs-Him and his fellow enlistees were known by the Indians of the plains as "wolves." They were well qualified to perform the tasks of scouts, having been trained since childhood in the proper techniques. Among the Crow, the wolves were called upon to scout enemy villages and read the signs, including watching animals to see if they would reveal an approaching enemy by their movement or manners. "A real wolf watches everything that moves. So must a human wolf or scout."

Often, White-Man-Runs-Him would paint his face, ears, arms and body with mud. When the mud dried it produced a whitish-gray color similar to the coat of a wolf. Sometimes the scouts would wear a wolf skin over their shoulders and back, with the wolf's head pulled down over their eyes to hide their faces from view.

When in the field, they sometimes crept like wolves moving very carefully. They even signaled each other through wolflike whines and howls. Many times the wolf scout went on his mission without the benefit of weapons. Each wolf group that went out on a mission had a pipe carrier. The guide and leader of the Crow scouts now under Gibbon's command was Half Yellow Face. These scouts had many signs and signals which they used to warn or signal each other. Special signals were designed to signal the U.S. troops for whom they were now scouting. One such technique called for the scouts to turn their horses in circles to warn of the approaching enemy.

Gibbon's unit did not offer the Crow scouts any weapons. Each scout brought his own weapon under the enlistment arrangements. White-Man-Runs-Him carried a breech-loading carbine, as did all but two of the Crow volunteers. He recalled, "Of the two without carbines, one had a revolver and the other a bow and arrow."

SOURCES

Chapter VI

Bradley, Lt. James H. *Montana Column*. Norman: University of Oklahoma, 1962. Edited by Edgar I. Stewart.
Enlistment of the Crows and events of the campaign.

Dixon, Joseph K. *The Vanishing Race*. New York: Popular Library, 1923.
Statement on enlistment.

Linderman, Frank B. *Plenty Coups*. Lincoln and London: University of Nebraska Press, 1930.
Plenty Coups' dream.

Medicine Crow, Joseph. Personal interview.
18 June 1990. *The role of White-Man-Runs-Him.*

Medicine Crow, Joseph. *Medicine Crow*. Lodge Grass, Montana: Crow Central Education Commission, 1979.
Contains the visions of Medicine Crow.

Stewart, Edgar I. *Custer's Luck*. Norman: University of Oklahoma Press, 1957.
Weapons of the scouts.

Willert, James. *Little Big Horn Diary*. Whittier: Spectrum Silk Screen, 1977.
Events on the campaign.

VII. WITH GIBBON

With the needed scouts in hand, and in relatively good spirits, Bradley packed up and moved out of the Agency toward their base camp on the Yellowstone River. White-Man-Runs-Him recalled that the small group had to move very slowly because the melting snow had turned the trail into mud. That night the tired soldiers got a surprise. It seems that a number of friends and relatives had followed the convoy to participate with the scouts in a dance designed to prepare them for the campaign and to wish them good fortune. The dance lasted well into the night and members of the command complained the next day about their lack of sleep.

Culture shock confronted White-Man-Runs-Him and his fellow scouts when Bradley ordered them out for roll-call the next morning. This was the first experience most of the Crow had with military procedure, and they didn't care for it. The younger scouts complained to their older counterparts, who tried to intervene with Gibbon about the military "restrictions." While some restrictions were eased, the general rules of the military would continue to frustrate the scouts, who were individuals in every way, including the way they waged war. The Crow were used to coming and going whenever they pleased. In some cases, they went out as individuals to hunt or to scout. White-Man-Runs-Him believed that their comings and goings became more frequent than normal because of the camp restrictions. On May 1, six Crow returned to the Agency. Bradley was very upset with the withdrawal and sent a message back to the Agency with an appeal for their return.

Each day, White-Man-Runs-Him scouted as he was commissioned to do, although there was little or no evidence of hostile activities in the area. On April 21, when the Gibbon forces were camped two miles above Fort Pease, Gibbon received a message from St. Paul headquarters that Crook would not take the field until the middle of May, and due to heavy snows, the Dakota column would not leave before that time either. The dispatch informed Gibbon that the Sioux were out in much greater numbers than had been originally estimated. This meant that Gibbon's command was without support in hostile territory. General Terry, therefore, ordered Gibbon to stay at abandoned Fort Pease until further notice.

On April 24, Captain Ball was ordered to take two troops of cavalry and scouts up the Big Horn as far as Fort C. F. Smith, which was located some 75 miles from the mouth of the Big Horn River. On their return, at almost the exact location where the Sioux and Cheyenne village was later located during Custer's battle, Jack Rabbit Bull, one of the Crow scouts, left a sign. He took a discarded bread box and, using a piece of charcoal, covered it with multiple signs which would let the Sioux know that the Crow and the soldiers intended to clean them out. He then took a handful of green grass and stuck it in the cracks of the box, which would tell the Sioux what the soldiers intended to do during the coming summer.

Jack Rabbit Bull left signs promising to wipe out the Sioux.

An embarrassing incident for White-Man-Runs-Him, the Crow scouts, and the soldiers as well, occurred on May 2. During the afternoon, a windstorm came up reducing visibility significantly. The next morning it was discovered that a horse and mule staked just outside the sentries post, about 100 yards from the main camp, were missing. Fearing the worst, White-Man-Runs-Him and several other scouts raced to the place where their horses were grazing just above the camp. When they reached the spot where they should be able to see where the horses were, there were none. The Sioux and Cheyenne presence had been verified. All 32 of the Crow horses were gone. White-Man-Runs-Him returned to the camp, and as the Crow scouts assembled, they were informed of the enemy's success. Together they began to wail and cry. They were not only letting off steam, but they were bemoaning their tremendous loss. They were weeping because their pride had been injured, and in one sense they had been defeated. They wept to gain power, they sang death songs, and they prayed to regain their strength.

For about a month after the horse raid, carried out by Two Moons of the Cheyenne, White-Man-Runs-Him and his tribal friends had to scout on foot through all types of difficult terrain. While Gibbon attempted to encourage the Crow to form a party to go after the horse thieves, he did not totally understand their culture and their views. Since the Crow were known as the best of the horse thieves, they would have to recover their horses or get new ones in their own way when they felt like it and when their medicine was right. Weather conditions and a variety of other religious factors would have to be favorable before an attempted recovery could take place. Then, too, the enemy would have to be present to make a recovery possible.

Because of his good humor, White-Man-Runs-Him was popular among the white soldiers. Perhaps because of his pleasant temperament, he was teased and kidded more than the other scouts about the loss of their horses. In his own words, "The remarks were ignored, and I marched with pride, my rifle over my shoulder."

Several days later Half Yellow Face and Jack Rabbit Bull, on borrowed cavalry horses, encountered three Sioux who were dismounted. They were able to drive the Sioux off and captured their horses. Scouting on foot was a difficult task; nevertheless, White-Man-

Runs-Him had great pride, was well-conditioned, and continued to scout with great success. In early May, he discovered fresh pony tracks and an abandoned village. This proved that the Sioux and their allies, the Cheyenne, had crossed to the North bank of the Yellowstone River. While discovering the village, he and his comrades came upon a small buffalo herd and killed several for fresh meat. Even though the fresh meat was greatly appreciated by Gibbon's forces, Bradley was concerned the shooting would alert the enemy. The Crow found this hard to understand, since they thought they had come on this venture to engage the Sioux.

As a result of the discovery of an enemy presence, Gibbon decided on May 8 to move his command down the river, based on the assumption that the Sioux and Cheyenne would be further to the east. The number of horse-riding scouts increased when the six Crow scouts who had left the command early in May returned with Barney Bravo and Little Face, on May 12. Gibbon now decided to encourage the discovery of enemy villages by offering bonuses. This caused the scouts to increasingly go out alone or in small groups, venturing further and further from the main camp.

On the morning of the 16th, White-Man-Runs-Him and several other scouts discovered a village of about 400 lodges with an estimated 800 to 1000 warriors. The village was located about 18 miles from the confluence of the Tongue and Yellowstone Rivers. When the location of the village was reported to Gibbon, he decided to attack. He prepared to cross the Yellowstone with five companies of infantry and four troops of cavalry, a total of 350 men and 34 officers.

White-Man-Runs-Him reported that the attempted crossing of the swollen river was a disaster. Accident after accident occurred, with several animals drowning in the rough stream. The attempted crossing was only able to move across 10 horses per hour. Gibbon now decided to cancel his planned attack. White-Man-Runs-Him was very upset, as were the other Crow scouts. They were looking forward to the attack as an opportunity to replace their stolen horses. Remembering the conversations at the recruiting council, the Crow openly questioned the white man's courage. They believed that only "Gibbon's cowardice" prevented them from a victory in which they would have acquired horses and again be mounted.

On the 19th of May, while scouting, White-Man-Runs-Him's contingent discovered a group of Army couriers who were searching for Gibbon. They were guided back to the camp where their message revealed that Terry was in the field with the entire Seventh Cavalry, and he would make contact with Gibbon in about a month. Gibbon was ordered to continue to patrol the river's north bank.

White-Man-Runs-Him noted that the signs of Sioux in the area continued to increase. Often the scouts saw Sioux "wolves" on their scouting missions. On a number of occasions, White-Man-Runs-Him was close enough to the enemy scouts that he was able to talk to them using sign language and the Sioux words that he knew. Discussions with the Sioux indicated they were hungry and gathering food for their families. It was obvious to White-Man-Runs-Him that the Sioux were moving north of the river in great numbers. A group of Crow found an interesting sign while on patrol — an arrow shaft broken in the middle and carefully laid on the ground. After much discussion with the elder Crow leaders, it was concluded that this meant, "I have quit fighting." They agreed the person who had placed the sign was not a Sioux, but rather a potential Sioux ally who decided to return to his home tribe.

Even now, White-Man-Runs-Him said the scouts were concerned about whether there were enough soldiers to handle the Sioux should a battle take place. On May 23, the scouts came across the scalped remains of two troopers and one cart driver from their own command. They had gone antelope hunting without permission and had been discovered by the Sioux.

On May 27, White-Man-Runs-Him, Bouyer, and LeForge were scouting in the Wolf Mountains. Ten days earlier when they had looked through the Valley of the Rosebud they saw nothing. Now White-Man-Runs-Him noticed smoke. When the scouts moved to a better position, they could see heavy smoke in many columns hanging like a blanket over the valley. The horse herd was of significant size and the village scattered over an area estimated to be about two miles. The scouts returned to inform Gibbon. Again, White-Man-Runs-Him and the Crow hoped for and expected an immediate attack, but it was not to be. Gibbon decided not to attack that day. The Crow speculated that the attack did not take place because the white forces "feared for themselves." Other opinion is that Gibbon did not want the tribes, who appeared to be gathering, to suddenly scatter. Gibbon's response was to send volunteers downstream in a skiff to look for General Terry, who was believed to be camped at the mouth of Glendive Creek on the Powder River.

The next day another Mackinaw boat appeared with supplies, including whiskey and champagne cider. There was also mail with new orders from Terry, which detailed his belief that the Indians were gathering above Glendive Creek. Gibbon was ordered to march along the north bank of the Yellowstone toward that point, then to cross the river and cooperate with the Dakota column. While both Bradley and Gibbon disagreed with Terry on the exact location of the Sioux Indians, they had no choice but to obey orders.

As Gibbon's forces prepared to move out, two Crow scouts along with Barney Bravo returned from a trip to the Crow Agency. They brought back horses for everyone except White-Man-Runs-Him and Goes Ahead. The latter two scouts refused to send back for more horses because of their pride and the belief that they would soon be able to take Sioux horses.

The Montana Column began its descent over the difficult terrain into the Yellowstone River Valley. Captain Clifford and several Crow scouts returned from a successful mission, having found the steamer, the "Far West," at the mouth of the Powder River. Soon the white scout Herendeen and another Crow scout came in with new orders from Terry requesting that Gibbon leave his troops in place and meet with Terry as he moved up the Yellowstone on the "Far West." White-Man-Runs-Him and two or three other scouts accompanied Gibbon downstream, where Gibbon met with Terry on June 9. As they continued to move upstream, Bradley and White-Man-Runs-Him followed the shore. After about a two-hour discussion, Gibbon left the boat with orders to retrace his steps to the camp opposite the mouth of the Rosebud. Terry returned on the boat to the mouth of the Powder River, where he had set up his base camp.

Upon his return, Gibbon ordered his command to break camp. They arrived at their rendezvous place on June 14, and the scouts continued to work up and down the river. There was still a great deal of speculation as to where the Sioux might be, and everyone waited for General Terry to reveal his plan.

On June 14, Terry ordered General Custer to take six companies of the Seventh Cavalry and head for the Tongue River to look for further evidence of the Sioux and Cheyenne. Custer was off on the 15th, while Terry, with a company of infantry, followed the "Far West." About 15 miles from the Powder River, the steamer broke down. The boat was quickly repaired and Terry joined Custer at his camp on June 16. White-Man-Runs-Him, Elk, and Two Whistles rode on the "Far West" for a short period of time, then returned to Gibbon, perhaps with a message from Terry.

From June 17 to the 19, Generals Terry and Custer waited for word from Reno, who was sent out to the mouth of the Rosebud. When Reno's scout came in, he said he had found a trail indicating a large force of Indians moving toward the valley of the Little Big Horn. Terry speculated that since no "hostiles" had been found on the Tongue or Powder Rivers, they must be somewhere on the Rosebud, Little Big Horn, or Big Horn Rivers.

On June 20, Terry ordered Custer to cross the Tongue and join forces with Reno and the rest of the Seventh. After taking on supplies from the "Far West," he marched to the Rosebud River with the entire command. Terry followed Custer, reaching Reno's camp about noon. Terry rested, then marched to Gibbon's camp at the mouth of the Rosebud on June 21.

That afternoon, Terry called a conference of his officers on the "Far West." The meeting lasted from 3:00 in the afternoon until sundown. Gibbon was extremely upset when he was informed that it was Custer who would have the first opportunity to strike a blow against the Sioux Indians. Gibbon reasoned that since he had been in the field since February 22, he and his men deserved the opportunity. Gibbon's men had come to regard the Yellowstone Indians as theirs. Gibbon must have understood, however, that Custer not only had more men than he did, but also had all the cavalry, giving him a decided advantage if the Indians decided to run, which it was generally accepted they would do.

Gibbon's problems increased when he was told that his six best scouts were to be dispatched to Reno's command under Custer. It was Bradley's responsibility to carry out the order, which he did by sending Bouyer up river to Gibbon's camp with instructions to bring back the scouts on the "Far West." Bradley recorded the following regret: "I selected my six best men, and they joined him [Custer] at the mouth of Rosebud...Our guide, Mitch Bouyer, accompanies him also. This leaves us wholly without a guide, while Custer has one of the very best that this country affords. Surely he is being offered every facility to make a successful pursuit."

The Crow scouts were brought to the south bank of the Yellowstone on the "Far West," where they were conducted immediately to Custer's tent. Their names were White-Man-Runs-Him, Goes Ahead, Half Yellow Face, White Swan, and Curley, the youngest, "about 17 summers in age." Mitch Bouyer served as their interpreter when they were introduced to their new leader, George Armstrong Custer. White-Man-Runs-Him recalled, "I was the first one of the Crows to shake hands with General Custer. He gripped me by the right hand and said, 'You are the one I want to see, and I am glad that you are first.' White-Man-Runs-Him's reputation had preceded him. Goes Ahead recalled that Custer shook hands with them and said, "We are glad to have you. We sent for you and you came right away." Through Bouyer, Custer gave the Crow scouts a briefing, explaining that he was going to fight the Dakotas and Cheyenne and that he understood the Crows were good scouts. "If we win the fight, everything belonging to the enemy you can take home, for my boys have no use for these things." He also told them: "I have called you Indians here not to fight, but to trace the enemy and tell me where they are; I do not want you to fight. You find the Indians and I will do the fighting." The Crows were apparently impressed with Custer. As Curley recalled: "When I saw Custer...tall and slim, with broad shoulders and kind eyes, I said to myself: 'There is a kind, brave, and thinking man.'" Goes Ahead remembered: "...I saw that General Custer was a man of about six feet two inches, slim and well-built, and kindhearted."

The Crow called Custer, "Son of the Morning Star." They had seen General Crook, whom they dubbed as "Morning Star," and for some unclear reason, they believed that Custer was Crook's son.

Maybe the Crow thought Crook and Custer looked alike, or maybe it was because Crook outranked Custer at the time, so that if he was Morning Star, then Custer was second to him, his son. In Crow religious tradition, Old Woman's grandson was the Sun's son, who after conquering various monsters on earth, returned to the sky to become the Morning Star. Some Crow prayed to the Morning Star in times of war and even erected sweat lodges to him during critical times. Could Crook, the first to engage the Sioux, have been seen by the Crow as representing Morning Star, the deity who was to rid the monsters, the Sioux, from the earth?

Custer, Son of the Morning Star, took an immediate liking to the Crows, not for what he thought they could do for him (though this, of course, was their purpose), but because of their remarkable physical appearance. He wrote to his wife Elizabeth about the Crow the same evening he met them: "...I now have some Crow scouts with me, as they are familiar with the country. They are magnificent looking men, so much handsomer and more Indian-like than any we have ever seen, and so jolly and sportive; nothing of the gloomy, silent redmen about them. They have formally given themselves to me, after the usual talk. In their speech, they said they had heard that I never abandoned a trail, that when my food gave out, I ate mule. That was the kind of man they wanted to fight under; they were willing to eat mule, too!"

SOURCES

Chapter VII

Dixon, Joseph K. *The Vanishing Race.* New York: Popular Library, 1923.
The scouts are introduced to Custer.

LeForge, Thomas. *Memoirs of a White Crow Indian.* Lincoln and London: University of Nebraska, 1974.
The expedition and agreement with White-Man-Runs-Him on the battlefield burial.

Lowie, Robert. "The Religion of the Crow." *Anthropological Papers.* American Museum of Natural History, Vol. XXV, 1922.
On the Morning Star.

Plenty Hoops, Winona. Personal interview.
13 June 1991. *Verifies White-Man-Runs-Him and LeForge story of Custer and battlefield burial, and events with Gibbon.*

Medicine Crow, Joseph. Personal interview.
15 June 1991. *Explained the role of White-Man-Runs-Him with Gibbon.*

Bradley, Lt. H. *Montana Column.* Norman: University of Oklahoma, 1961.
G98
edited by Edgar I. Stewart
Day-by-day with Gibbon.

Willert, James. *Little Big Horn Diary.* Whittier: Spectrum Silk Screen, 1977.
Day-by-day accounts.

VIII. THE SIGNS AND POWER OF MEDICINE PROPHESY CUSTER'S DEFEAT

Members of the Sioux and Northern Cheyenne tribes gathered together on the banks of the Rosebud, not more than 12 miles north of the present-day Cheyenne Agency at Lame Deer, to participate in their annual Sun Dance. The dance, which began on June 13, 1876, had been vowed by Sitting Bull for the Hunkpapa Sioux. He would be the primary dancer on that day.

Sometime earlier, Sitting Bull, following the traditional practice of the Sioux, declared to the Creator, before witnesses and facing the sun, that he would participate in the Sun Dance for two days and two nights. He declared that he would kill a buffalo and make a sacrifice to the Creator. His prayers petitioned for food for his people so they would not face hunger during the winter, and he prayed for more power for the Sioux, so the nation might be strong and successful. Finally, he sought a good heart for his people so that they would be happy and live well together.

Shortly after his vow, Sitting Bull shot the promised buffalo and staked it out with each leg pointing in one of the four directions. When the sacrifice to the Great Mystery had been completed, the Sun Dance began.

While Sitting Bull had participated in the Sun Dance a number of times before, he decided on this occasion to give 100 pieces of his flesh. An awl was used to lift the skin from the body where it was cut off by a knife. Skin was taken from his wrist to his shoulder on each arm. Those gathered to watch saw his arms bleed, then clot, and finally close.

Sitting Bull began to dance. He danced all day and all night. Around noon of the next day, he became tired and faint. Black Moon, the intercessor for the dance, walked out to where Sitting Bull was dancing, took hold of him, and helped him to lie down. Sitting Bull spoke softly for some time to Black Moon as he lay exhausted on the ground. Black Moon finally stood up and called out to all who were observing that the vision had been completed, the offerings accepted, and the prayers of Sitting Bull had been heard. Black Moon shouted that the voices had told Sitting Bull, "I give you these because they have no ears." In his vision Sitting Bull had looked up where he saw soldiers and Indians coming down like grasshoppers, with their heads down and their hats falling off. "They were falling right into the Sioux camp. These dead soldiers were interpreted to be the gifts of the Creator. Kill them, but do not take their guns or horses. Do not touch these spoils, for if you set your hearts upon these goods of the white man, it will prove a curse to this nation."

When the vision had been heard, the Sioux and Cheyenne encampments were in good spirits and their hearts were filled with joy. The prophesy of the dream was clear. The soldiers would come, but they were coming in upside down. They would be defeated and the promise of the Great Mystery thus would be fulfilled.

On the afternoon of June 22, just nine days after the Sun Dance, Custer left the main camp on the Rosebud River. With trumpeters playing, the regiment was paraded out of camp as they marched to their fate. White-Man-Runs-Him, Mitch Bouyer, and the other Crow scouts were well in front of the Seventh Cavalry and led the way. Between the Crow and the Custer forces were the Arikara scouts that Custer had brought with him from North Dakota. They were divided into two groups, one led by Bobtailed Bull and the other by Soldier. One group covered each bank of the river.

That night White-Man-Runs-Him selected a camp at the base of a bluff. The spot was selected because the Crow knew it contained an adequate supply of grass for the animals, as well as providing plenty of water and wood. That evening a number of officers and enlisted men went fishing.

Once the camp had been selected, the scouts left to do their work. When they returned later that evening, White-Man-Runs-Him, Half Yellow Face, Bouyer, and Lt. Godfrey discussed the day's work using sign language, with Bouyer interpreting for Godfrey. Godfrey was asked by Half Yellow Face if he had ever fought these Sioux. Lt. Godfrey nodded that he had. He then told the scouts he believed there would be about 1500 warriors. Bouyer asked Godfrey, "Do you think we can whip that many?" The scouts listened intently with a solemn expression as Godfrey again answered in the affirmative. Bouyer then told Godfrey, "Well, I can tell you we are going to have a damned big fight."

On June 23, Custer camped within one-half mile of Sitting Bull's Sun Dance site. On June 24, when Custer's troops arrived at the abandoned encampment, they noticed the signs of the Sun Dance circle. A white man's scalp hung in the center of the Sun Dance lodge framework. A buffalo calfskin tied to four poles with cloth and other articles of religious significance were nearby. It was obvious to the

A scalp hung in the center of the Sun Dance Lodge. A buffalo calfskin tied to four poles was nearby. In one of the sweat lodges was a mound of sand showing the two forces facing each other. Dead men were drawn with their heads facing the Indian soldiers.

Crow and the Arikara scouts that big medicine had been made on this spot.

White-Man-Runs-Him and his fellow scouts returned from their duties to the main camp on the right bank of the Rosebud about 6:00 A.M. on the 24th. White-Man-Runs-Him was anxious to observe the Sun Dance signs, for he had heard of its power. That very day he had talked at some distance by sign language with scouts of the Sioux and Cheyenne, and they had told him that great things had been done at the Sun Dance camp.

The Crow and Arikara scouts, along with Custer's soldiers, observed that the sand in several areas had been moved and replaced in a certain way at selected spots, so that pictures could be drawn in it. In one of the sweat lodges there was a mound of sand showing hoof prints of soldiers on one side and the Indian warriors on the other. Dead men were drawn with their heads facing the Indian forces. After some discussion, the Crow and Arikara agreed that the signs showed

The scouts believed that this sign foretold a Sioux victory.

that the Sioux and Cheyenne knew the soldiers were on their way, that their medicine was strong, and that the Indians would defeat the white army.

Another piece of evidence of Sioux confidence in their power was two buffalo skulls, one bull, the other a cow, facing one another with a pile of rocks in the middle. A stick pointed in the direction of the cow. To the scouts this meant that when they were overtaken, the Sioux and Cheyenne would fight like a bull and the white soldiers would retreat like "women."

As the Seventh Cavalry began to move out, they noticed inscriptions on the sandstone located on the right bank of the Rosebud. One sign showed a smaller buffalo charging a larger one. Between the buffalo was a shaft of stone. The scouts concluded that the smaller buffalo represented Custer and the stone symbolized the Badlands country. The larger Indian party was withdrawing into their country where they would fight to the end. The scouts agreed that the sign meant they should not follow the Dakotas into the Big Horn country, "For they will turn and destroy us."

While the officers met, Custer's flag fell over. It was set up again, but blew down a second time. Many who observed the incident feared it was a sign of the battle to come.

While Custer and his officers prepared for a meeting, another interesting event took place. When Custer's flag was placed in the ground, it fell over. When it was set up again, it fell down a second time. Some of the soldiers and scouts viewed the unusual occurrence with wonder, even concern. Discussions focused on whether or not this could be a bad sign, forecasting defeat in the battle to come.

Further investigation by the scouts revealed a sweat lodge containing three stones, painted red, and lined up in a row near the middle of the dwelling. According to Crow interpretation, this meant the Great Mystery had already given the Sioux and Cheyenne victory, and if the army did not come after them, then they would pursue the army.

The troopers moved out once again, and after a short ride took a coffee break at approximately 1:00 P.M. They were located about four miles north of Lame Deer, within a few miles of Deer Medicine Rock, a holy place possessing powerful medicine. It was at Medicine Rock where the Cheyenne chiefs also saw visions of the impending battle with the soldiers. An ancient Cheyenne legend holds that, "One who defaces Deer Medicine Rock will not have long to live." Some time after the troopers had been in the area, the Cheyenne would discover four names deeply carved into the rock. While time would prove that several of the names were soldiers' names, they were not members of the Seventh Cavalry. The Cheyenne had no way of knowing whose names had been carved in the rock, and so when Custer was killed, they rejoiced, believing that the rock had released its power on behalf of the Cheyenne.

The Cheyenne had, however, placed a curse directly on Custer several years earlier. Following his unprovoked massacre of Black Kettle's Southern Cheyenne camp on the Washita River in Oklahoma on November 27, 1869, Custer captured more than 50 Indian women and children. Among the captives was a girl under 20 years of age named Monahseetah, the daughter of the deceased Chief Little Rock. Custer developed a great interest in her and had her assigned to his headquarters tent as an interpreter, even though she could not speak English.

Monahseetah traveled with the Seventh Cavalry as far as Texas during one of Custer's campaigns. Sioux and Cheyenne oral histories

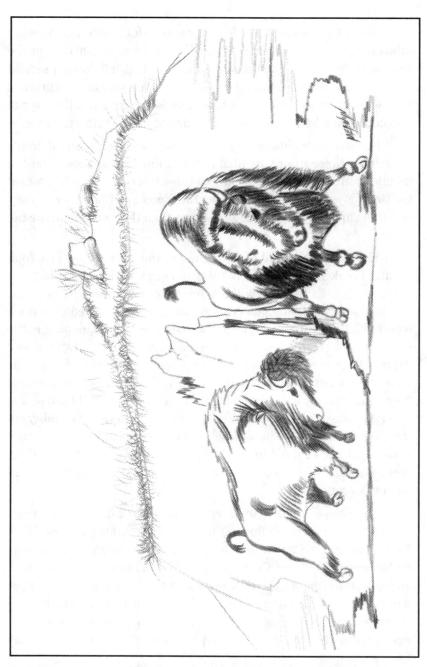

As Custer's troops moved out they noticed inscriptions on the sandstone. The scouts agreed that the Sioux were predicting that the smaller buffalo representing Custer would be defeated by the larger buffalo representing the Sioux.

Deer Medicine Rock. Near this holy place, the Cheyenne gathered for ceremonies. It was here that the visions of the Chiefs predicted a Custer defeat.

have long declared that Yellow Hair [Custer] was the father of Monahseetah's son, whom she named Yellow Swallow, although some historians believe Yellow Swallow to be the child of a Cheyenne warrior.

When Yellow Swallow was about seven years old, he and his mother were in the Southern Cheyenne camp when Custer came to discuss peace. On that particular day, Brave Bear, a powerful Medicine Man, was in charge of the pipe, lighting it, then smoking it first and last. As the conference began, Brave Bear recalled in his mind the humiliation to Monahseetah, her rejection by Custer when his wife arrived at the Seventh Cavalry camp, and the fact that no Cheyenne would now marry her. With this in mind, Brave Bear asked Custer to remove one boot, which he did. Into the boot he poured the ashes from the pipe (some legends say the ashes were put on Custer's boot). As smoke rose from the boot, Brave Bear told Custer, "If you ever break your vow of good will and eternal peace, this will happen to you. It will not be the Cheyennes who do it. It will be of your own doing." Thus Custer had placed upon him the endless curse of the Everywhere Spirit. The Cheyenne medicine was powerful. The prophecies would soon be fulfilled.

Back on the trail, White-Man-Runs-Him along with his companion scouts, reported to Custer that they had observed many large abandoned Sioux camps ahead. The trail left by the enemy as they broke camp was over one-half mile wide. White-Man-Runs-Him also reported that beards and scalps of white men were scattered throughout one of the main encampments.

While the Crow scouts went to get something to eat, Custer decided to confer with the Arikara. His flag bearer was with him. They found the Arikara sitting in a half-circle, with Stabbed and Red Bear, the leaders, sitting together. Custer sat down with one knee on the ground and inquired as to whether or not the Arikara agreed with the Crow report that there were large Sioux camps ahead with many warriors present. Before anyone in the Arikara circle had a chance to speak Custer asked, "What do you suppose will be the outcome of it all?"

Stabbed jumped up and hopped about the fire, pretending to dodge the bullets of the Sioux. The entire gathering watched as Stabbed finally came to a stop appearing ready to speak. He addressed Custer: "Chief, this is a part of our tactics. When we dodge about this way, we make it hard for the enemy to hit us. We have learned from the Sioux that they have shot you whites down like buffalo calves. You stand in rows, erect, and do not dodge about, so it is easy to shoot you."

After Stabbed sat down he said to Scout Frank Gerard, who had joined the gathering, "I want you to tell Custer that I showed him how we fight, for when his soldiers go into the fight they stand still like targets while the Sioux are dodging about so it is hard to hit them. But they shoot the soldiers down very easily."

Custer replied that he didn't doubt what Stabbed said, that it seem reasonable. "I know your people; you are tricky like the coyote, you know how to hide, to creep up and take by surprise." Other officers now began to gather around the activities of the Arikara fire.

As the discussion continued, Custer revealed his plan for the Arikara, "My only intention in bringing these people [Arikara] to battle is to have them go into battle and take many horses away from the Sioux." Custer extended his arms and told the group he was glad and pleased to have so many familiar faces with him on this expedition. "Some of you I see here have been with me on one or two other expeditions, and to see you again makes my heart glad. And on this expedition if we are victorious, when we return home, Bloody Knife, Bob-Tailed Bull, Soldier, Strikes Two, and Stabbed will be proud to have following behind them on parade marches those who have shown themselves to be brave young men. When your chief sees you on parade, I am sure he will be proud to see his boys."

Custer then turned to Gerard and said, "I want you to tell these young men, these boys, that if we are successful, when we return, my brother, Bloody Knife, and I will represent you at Washington and perhaps we will take you in person to Washington." While Custer seemed to speak with confidence, some of the men who listened to him speak began to wonder if the Crow reports concerning the vast numbers of Sioux warriors were bothering him. His dialogue seemed to raise some doubts about victory.

After they finished eating, the Crow scouts rested for a few minutes before starting out again to track the prints of the lodge pole travois to see where they led. After being on the trail for some time, White-Man-Runs-Him discovered that the new marks swung over to the Rosebud and joined the main trail. The signs indicated that it was at this point that many groups were joining the main force. Those joining proved to be Agency Indians. The numbers of the Sioux and Cheyenne continued to grow. With this new information, the scouts returned to Custer, where they again reported the force before them was of tremendous proportions.

While White-Man-Runs-Him and the Crow scouts rested, Custer began to advance across the Rosebud to the left bank. Aware that the Sioux were not far ahead, the Seventh Cavalry was ordered to slow down the pace. The Crow did not rest long before they mounted their horses, caught up with the troopers, and moved out into the lead. The terrain was dusty and increasingly difficult to master. Signs were everywhere that an extremely large pony herd was being driven over the valley trail. White-Man-Runs-Him and his partners were ordered to check out all trails to the left. Custer was convinced the Sioux might somehow escape around his left flank.

The Crow recommended that camp be made at a spot located a few miles from the present town of Busby, Montana. Custer was only about 22 miles east of the Little Big Horn. While camp was being set up, White-Man-Runs-Him, Goes Ahead, and Hairy Moccasin were sent ahead to see where the trail led. White-Man-Runs-Him noted the Sioux had crossed the divide, but the scouts were unable to discover the exact location of the camp. When they returned to the Busby camp, White-Man-Runs-Him told Varnum that he went to a high peak, but was not sure if the Sioux were on the Little Big Horn or not. It was late and he could not see very well. One thing was certain; the Indian camp had not broken up. They were still together and since they hadn't turned north toward Tullock's Fork, nor south to the main Rosebud, they must have gone up Davis Creek and would most likely be in the vicinity of the Little Big Horn.

Custer wanted to know exactly where the camp was. He therefore decided to issue a new order to White-Man-Runs-Him and the other Crow scouts. They were to follow the trail through the night until they had the exact location of the village. If they discovered nothing by noon of the June 25, they were to return to the command post. In Custer's words, "Tonight you shall go without sleep. You are to go ahead. You are to try to locate the Sioux camp. You are to do your best to find this camp. Travel all night. When day comes, if you have not found the Sioux camp, keep on going until noon. If your search is useless by this time, you are to come back to camp."

White-Man-Runs-Him knew this land better than anyone. This land of the buffalo, deer, sunshine, rain, and snow was Crow land, his land. The Crow scouts now discussed Custer's orders and offered a plan designed to save time. They told Custer about a place on the Rosebud divide from where the Crow had many times observed the Little Big Horn Valley when planning war against the Sioux. After dawn, when the air was clear, the valley could be seen. If the Sioux were in the valley, their smoke would be seen; if not, the trail could be followed. Custer wanted to know how far away the lookout was. White-Man-Runs-Him told Custer he thought about two hours. He added that there was also a place to hide the horses. The scouts noted that if they left right away they could reach the lookout before daylight.

Custer accepted the plan. The scouts took a brief rest, then left camp at about 9:30 P.M. The scouts included White-Man-Runs-Him, Goes Ahead, Hairy Moccasin, White Swan, Curley, Lt. Varnum, Charlie Reynolds, and 10 Arikara. Custer decided to move his column at 11:00 P.M. and head for the base of the mountain, where he would await a report from the scouts.

White-Man-Runs-Him was the lead scout. They followed the trail from the Rosebud River across to the Little Horn. White-Man-Runs-Him was now riding a cavalry horse. They pushed themselves and their horses hard as they raced through the moonless darkness. Stopping for a rest, the Crow indicated that by daybreak they would reach a high point where "they could see far: from it all, the hills would seem to go down flat."

When they arrived at the Crow's Nest, it was around 2:00 A.M., June 25. They led their horses into a sheltered draw behind the hill and waited until about an hour before dawn. White-Man-Runs-Him, Hairy Moccasin, and Goes Ahead climbed the lookout first, while the others in the party rested after riding the 12 or more miles in four hours over rough terrain.

With the sun just rising, Hairy Moccasin first sighted the smoke which engulfed the great camp some 12 to 15 miles away. It was Goes Ahead who first spotted the distant horses that appeared "like tiny maggots crawling on a fresh killed buffalo robe pegged out for scraping." White-Man-Runs-Him had a keen eye, having been trained as a youth for the action he was now engaged in. In his words, "We could make out smoke from the Sioux camp down in the Little Big Horn Valley and could see white horses on the other side of the Little Horn River..."

The three Crow now began to move down from their high position to their colleagues sleeping below. As they came to the camp, they used the "soft call of the owl" as their signal. White-Man-Runs-Him tapped the shoulders of the three sleeping Crow and the Arikara only to be surprised when the Arikara immediately broke into a mournful chanting of their death song. Using hand signs, White-Man-Runs-Him told them to be silent.

White-Man-Runs-Him thought the Arikara were brave enough when it came to fighting the Sioux, but they went to pieces making unnecessary noise to keep up their courage. To White-Man-Runs-Him, they were small, wiry, and dark-skinned compared to other Plains Indians. He felt that they were dirty and careless in their personal habits. It was difficult for him to understand how a man like Custer could have brought nearly 40 of them from Dakota.

Custer's favorite Arikara scout, Bloody Knife, was half Sioux and had a great weakness for battle. He was a "drinking buddy" of Custer's and was seen a number of times in a drunken condition while on the trail.

Curly related that when he first met Custer, the General expressed a concern about the Arikara when he said, "I have seen all the tribes but the Crows, and now I see them for the first time, and I think they are good and brave scouts. I have some scouts here, but they are worthless." White-Man-Runs-Him remembered that conversation and was concerned about what the Arikara might do.

White-Man-Runs-Him next awakened Varnum, Chief of the scouts and told him the village had been sighted. Varnum informed the Arikara, Crooked Horn, who then sent his scouts to the nest to see. They agreed the Sioux camp was where the Crow had indicated. Varnum ordered Crooked Horn to have someone ready to ride to inform Custer, who was waiting some 10 miles back. White-Man-Runs-Him thought the Arikara were very quick to seek the credit for the sighting.

Varnum and Reynolds scrambled up the hill to take a look. The Crow tried over and over again to help Varnum see, but all he could see was open terrain and two tepees. "They told me to look for worms," said Varnum, but his eyes were not trained for such work.

Varnum finally accepted the Crow's view that the village was sighted. White-Man-Runs-Him suggested to Varnum that Son-of-the-Morning-Star should come and see the enemy camp for himself. Reynolds scratched a quick note and gave it to the Arikara scouts, Red Star and Bull, to take to Custer.

As the Arikara left, at about 5:00 A.M., the Crow noticed smoke rising in the north and east. They became angry for they feared that the Sioux would now be warned of their immediate presence through this act of carelessness. The Crow were further concerned when, in White-Man-Runs-Him's words, "We saw two Sioux about one mile and a half west, moving down Davis Creek toward the soldiers' camp, and six other Sioux to the northeast over Tullock Fork..." The Arikara chased the six Sioux, but they escaped to the village. According to White-Man-Runs-Him, when the Sioux neared the camp, they began to circle their horses. There was now no doubt that the Sioux knew the soldiers were near.

It is interesting, that the night before the battle, Charlie Reynolds opened his warsack and divided its contents among his friends. Many had refused his presents, while the others accepted with reluctance. Charlie apparently had a premonition of either his fate, the troopers' fate, or both.

When the two Arikara scouts arrived at the Custer camp, they found many men lying in groups sleeping. While Red Star dismounted, the troops began to gather around him. Custer was down on one knee and asked if the Sioux had been sighted. Red Star nodded, then handed Custer the note from the Crow's Nest.

Custer was excited. He jumped on his horse bareback and rode throughout the camp speaking to his officers in a low voice, detailing the orders of the day. Custer then talked to Bloody Knife, who appeared to be in a state of depression. Bloody Knife expressed his view that there were over 5,000 Sioux, and he advised against the regiment being thrown at the large encampment.

By 8:30 A.M., Custer had the regiment ready to go. The scouts led off first with the troopers following shortly after. About an hour out, they came to a wooded ravine where they halted and concealed themselves. Custer went on to the Crow's Nest. When he arrived, he climbed the butte with Charlie Reynolds, who led him to the best lookout point. Custer told Reynolds he was imagining things. He said he saw nothing, no enemy camp. He looked again with glasses, then he did concede for a moment, "It's possible. You may be right."

With Mitch Bouyer at his side White-Man-Runs-Him sought to talk to Custer through Bouyer. White-Man-Runs-Him was angry because he didn't believe Custer was crediting the Crow for discovering the camp. With White-Man-Runs-Him squatting behind Custer, Bouyer asked Custer, "This Indian here wants to know what you think of the enemy camp?" Custer stated, "If there is an enemy camp out there, they haven't seen our army. None of their scouts have seen us." White-Man-Runs-Him then said, "You say we have not been seen. We saw two young Sioux going fast toward camp. They were close enough to see the smoke of your army's breakfast fires." Custer, now upset, returned: "I say again, we have not been seen. That camp has not sighted us."

Custer now was determined to carry out his plan. He said he would march after dark and surround the enemy from all sides. White-Man-Runs-Him reacted by saying, "That plan is no good. The Sioux may have already spotted your soldiers, and will report your coming to the camp." Custer, now angry, restated his plan. White-Man-Runs-Him spoke no more; he would do as ordered. He mounted his horse and joined his fellow Crow. Custer returned to his unit.

After Custer left, White-Man-Runs-Him, Varnum, and the other Crow noted a small group of Sioux Indians moving downstream. They believed the camp was breaking up and moving. In actuality, the camp was moving to join the larger village because they knew about the Custer forces.

When Custer came down from the Crow's Nest and returned to his command, his brother Tom ran toward him shouting, "They've spotted us. The Sioux know we are marching against them." Custer told his brother he was getting as "jumpy as the Crow," and that he didn't believe the column had been spotted.

During the regiment's advance, one of Captain Yates Company F pack mules lost a portion of the cargo. The pack mules had been behind during the entire trip. Now the pack mules had lost a box of hardtack. Sgt. William Curtis and a small detachment was sent back to find it. When they found the box, a Sioux boy, along with some friends, was sitting on the box eating some of the goods. His name was Deeds, the 10-year-old nephew of Sitting Bull. When the troopers saw him, they fired their carbines. A bullet hit him in the chest, killing him instantly. Two other boys ran away. The soldiers did not give pursuit, but the battle at Little Big Horn had begun.

Informed of the incident, Custer probably reasoned that the Crow had seen a village; several groups of Indians had been seen riding toward the large camp, and one group was chased by the Arikara; the Crow were worried Custer's smoke from his camp had been seen; and a boy had been shot after opening the hardtack box. Were the Sioux and Cheyenne watching his every move? Were they getting ready to attack? Were the numbers as great as the scouts said? Would his future hinge on his victory? Would the Indians run away? Would they fight?

Perhaps Custer remembered his own words, his own theory: "Indians will not attack and close with large bodies of troops; if attacked, Indians will only fight to escape." Whatever his thoughts were, Custer reacted, "Weapons inspection without delay. Change in plans. We will push on today and strike as soon as we find them."

Tom Custer ordered Varnum to have his scouts ready. Custer talked to his commanders, then requested a talk with the scouts. He spoke to them as he had before. When he first met the Crow, he told them, "I have called you not to fight but to trace the enemy and tell me where they are. I do not want you to fight. You will find the Indians and I will do the fighting."

Custer, through Gerard, called together the Arikaras, then told them, "Go straight for the camp, capture the horses; you will get experience today." They began to prepare for battle. They took off their dust-stained clothes, stripped to breechclouts and moccasins, and daubed their faces, arms, and chests with smears of powdered war paint, dampened with saliva. Eagle feathers were prepared and war songs began. Stabbed rubbed clay that he had brought from Fort Lincoln on each Arikara in hopes of assuring safety in the battle to come.

Privately, through Gerard, Custer told White-Man-Runs-Him, "I would rather die here today with the flag over me than return without orders." The Crow now readied themselves for battle. White-Man-Runs-Him painted sacred white clay stripes down his face. Half Yellow Face, the Crow pipe carrier, offered tobacco to the four winds. Mitch Bouyer told Half Yellow Face, "You and I are going home today by a trail that is strange to both of us."

The night before the battle, Sitting Bull wandered off to a ridge by himself. He prayed to the Great Spirit to hear and to pity him. He offered tobacco in the name of his people to save them and to guard them against misfortune. His earlier dream would soon be fulfilled. The Great Spirit had heard him and the power was with the Sioux and Cheyenne.

Custer's forces were ready to ride shortly before noon on June 25. Custer called White-Man-Runs-Him over to him. Mitch Bouyer rode up with him. Custer looked at him and said, "You know the country. Go ahead and look for me and see where I can make a success." It was White-Man-Runs-Him who was to lead the way.

He led the troops at a lope up the slope of the divide. Within a few minutes they reached the summit of the divide between the Rosebud and the Little Big Horn Rivers. Before them was the Valley of the Little Big Horn. From the summit they could see dust from the camp some 15 to 20 miles away. The column continued to ride in rows of fours at intervals of 50 or 60 feet. Custer called a halt for a brief conference in a valley surrounded by high hills. White-Man-Runs-Him said the day was hot and the horses were foaming and lathering as they drank in the slew. The cavalry was about 12 miles from the last camp. The pack mules were brought up at this stop and the troops were served whiskey.

George Curley, 61 or 62 year old grandson of Curley, related on November 10, 1975:

> I recall my grandfather often telling that during the march up the Rosebud he was dispatched with a message to the rear of the column. As he approached the main supply mules, he noticed a smaller outfit some distance back so he went there instead. Here some soldiers were drinking whiskey from a keg and he noticed that the six mules carried two small kegs, one on each side. The soldiers were filling their canteens. Then again, after the first sighting of the enemy camp and prior to the attack, the march down dense Ashwood Creek[Reno Creek] was halted. These same mules were brought up and the kegs were opened and whiskey poured into the cups of the soldiers. We scouts joined the line and drank the "bad water." Hairy Moccasin advised, "Do not drink the crazy water."

Robert Yellowtail, aged eighty seven, once a son-in-law of White-Man-Runs-Him, often repeated the old scout's version of one of the drinking halts:

> While coming down dense Ashwood Creek with the General and us scouts with Mitch Bouyer at the head of the column, Son-of-the-Morning-Star signalled a halt. While we were munching on hardtacks and bacon, pack mules were brought up quickly, each carrying small kegs, one on each side. These were unplugged and soldiers filed by with their cups to receive their share. We scouts joined in; before long my finger tips and lips tingled and felt numb. Our interpreter, Mitch Bouyer, explained that the whiskey was to make the soldiers brave.

Medicine Crow said that White-Man-Runs-Him told him that after the first quick drink, he spat the rest out as quickly as possible. George Curley continued his narrative:

> It was my personal observation on several occasions that White-Man-Runs-Him would become irritated or disgusted with interviewers who showed disinterest or incredibility when he mentioned the drinking incident. The same disinterest or incredibility was a reaction also shown by some interviewers to the other scouts, and some indicated that they were admonished by "influential people" to desist from saying that there was drinking by the soldiers.

Joe Medicine Crow agrees with the Curley's statement and recalled an incident when he and several of his friends were asked by White-Man-Runs-Him to act as interpreters during an interview with a writer. After some frustration, White-Man-Runs-Him told Medicine Crow, "Tell this man I don't like him. He asks leading questions. I am tired. I am insulted. When I tell the truth, he won't listen."

George Curley testified that his grandfather recalled "that when the Crow scouts sighted the Sioux camp, and one went back to tell the General, he soon came galloping madly up the high hill and after peering through his 'glasses' he dashed down the hill like a drunk man." Then later, as Custer veered off north from Reno's column, "he was already quite inebriated." This was a very serious charge coming from one of the five elite scouts of Custer.

Libby Custer, the General's wife, often stated that Custer hadn't taken a drink since his state of drunkenness when they first met.

White-Man-Runs-Him often stated that Bloody Knife and Custer were "drinking buddies." Pretty Shield, wife of Goes Ahead, said her husband told her Son of the Morning Star [Custer] drank too often from the straw covered bottle on his saddle. It is interesting to note that after the battle, Wooden Leg, a Cheyenne, reported having two bottles of whiskey which he recovered from the battle and passed among his friends. When the Cheyenne sung songs recounting their booty, one of the verses sung was, "I got whiskey."

After the battle, Sitting Bull was upset when some of the "Agency Indians, who got drunk on the whiskey found in the dead soldiers canteens, fired volley after volley of shots into the darkened night."

At the whiskey stop, Mitch Bouyer and Charlie Reynolds reported to Custer their recent findings. They stated that the smoke beyond the bluffs proved that the number of Indians beyond the bluffs was enormous. They told him the camp was at least a half-mile wide and extended for several miles. With that news, Custer was ready to move.

As Curley and Black Fox, along with several Arikara, left the command position between two small streams feeding Reno Creek, Custer decided to split his command. Benteen was ordered to take his three companies of 125 men and move to the south, then make a move to the left in oblique fashion. He was ordered to engage any enemy he might come across and to inform Custer if he was successful. It seemed to the scouts that Custer was going to drive any Indians who tried to escape back toward Benteen.

Mitch Bouyer, who always spoke his mind to Custer, again protested the division of the command. Bouyer told Custer something to the effect of , "if you don't find more Indians in that valley than you have ever saw before, you can hang me." Custer allegedly laughed and said, "All right, all right." Custer replied that "it would do a damned lot of good to hang you, wouldn't it?" Bouyer continued the exchange until Custer finally hollered to Bouyer, "I shall attack them. If you are afraid...," to which Custer's guide snapped in anger, "I can go wherever you can go, but if we go in there, we will never come out alive."

Bloody knife added as he looked up and made a gesture to the sun, "I shall not see you go down behind the mountains tonight."

White-Man-Runs-Him looking at Bloody Knife said, "Today we die, I go as a Crow."

Custer took five companies [225 men] with him, while Reno was assigned three companies of 112 men. Approximately 130 men, or about three companies, were assigned to the rear guard and pack escort.

As the troop left at a trot, Reno followed to Custer's left about 150 to 200 yards from Custer's cavalry on the left bank of Reno Creek, or, as the Crow called it, Ash Creek. Custer rode to the right side of the creek.

White-Man-Runs-Him reported that Custer moved rapidly down the creek, and it was difficult for the smaller Indian ponies to keep up the pace. After several miles, Reno's troops began to fall behind and with fatigue setting in for all, Custer again halted the command near some pine trees about four miles from the mouth of Reno Creek.

As the troops headed out again, the scouts were riding in and out reporting to Custer. Sometimes Custer would ride out by himself, look around, then return to the command. About 2:00 P.M., White-Man-Runs-Him and the other Crow scouts came to a halt. Just ahead was a lone Sioux tepee. A small fire smoldered and debris everywhere proved it had been a campsite not long ago.

White-Man-Runs-Him was familiar with the markings on the tepee. They were signs of death. The signs indicated a dead warrior was inside and the sacred symbols were to draw Wakan Tonkin's attention to the fleeting spirit and help insure its arrival in the spirit world. Time would reveal that it was Old She Bear, a warrior who had received mortal wounds in both hips fighting Crook on the Rosebud days earlier.

The Arikara had allowed the Crow lead the way to the tepee. When they realized that there was no immediate danger, they rushed to the tepee and lashed its cover and walls, then backed off to ponder their work. Finally after looking over the site, Red Feather, an Arikara, entered the lodge and drank some soup and ate some meat that had been left as a sacrifice. White-Man-Runs-Him was very upset with the Arikara behavior. "This would bring bad luck." As the group left, some soldiers started the tepee on fire. According to White-Man-

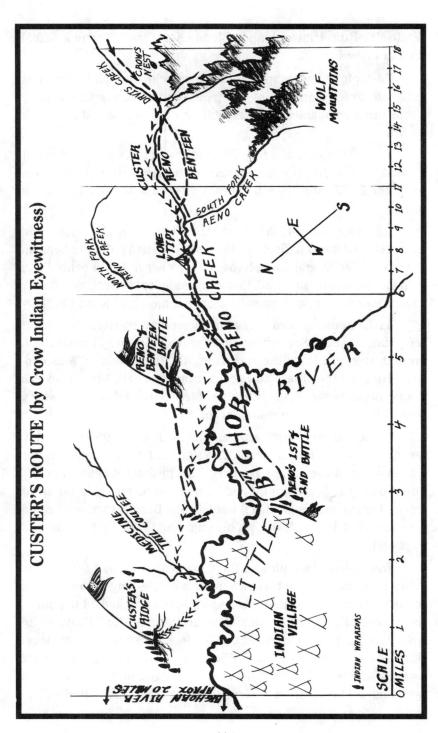

CUSTER'S ROUTE (by Crow Indian Eyewitness)

Runs-Him, this would bring even more bad luck. He was very upset; the Crow would not have done these things. The incident would bother him for the rest of his days and he would always correct historians who blamed the Crow for the desecration.

Not far from the tepee, Custer halted his troops. He ordered Reno to cross the tributary and the two columns were rejoined. Custer now asked White-Man-Runs-Him, who had been working ahead of the troopers, "Did you see any signs?" White-Man-Runs-Him answered in the affirmative. Then he pointed in the direction of the Sioux and Cheyenne camp and said, "Your friends are camped over there, and there are many. We should attack at night." Half Yellow Face replied that he disagreed.

Custer now spoke to the Arikara, "Boys, I want you to take the horses from the Sioux. Go straight to their camp and capture as many horses as possible. You're going to have a hard day of it." The scouts had already painted themselves and prepared for battle. Frank Gerard was ordered to get the Arikara moving. The Crow then noticed a rise of dust in the valley. Half Yellow Face shouted to Custer, "The Sioux must be running away."

The soldiers noticed 50 or more Indians between them and the Little Big Horn. The Sioux were covering the movement of a small village as it moved toward the big camp. Finally, the village was sighted by the troopers. Gerard shouted, "Here are your Indians running like devils." Custer ordered Lt. Hare to take White-Man-Runs-Him and the other Crow scouts and move ahead by the quickest way possible.

The Arikara still had not moved as ordered. Custer was angry and blasted the Arikara through Gerard with signs and voice. "I told you to dash on and stop for nothing! You have disobeyed me!" This had little effect, so he employed sarcasm and shame-arousing argument, "If any man of you is not brave, I will take away his weapon and make a woman of him!" Custer knew the male Indian's ego and the effect this threat would make upon them. The scouts caught his meaning, but made a defensive response through Gerard that was intended to soften their own guilt. "Tell him [Custer] if he does the same to all his white soldiers who are not so brave as we are, it will take him a very long time indeed!" The scouts all laughed at this and said by signs they were hungry for battle. But Custer was fed up with their "summer soldier" rhetoric, and ordered them again, through Gerard, to "...move to one side and let the soldiers pass you in the charge!"

In the same breath, he charged Lt. Cooke with instructions to Major Reno, who, with Lts. George Wallace and Benny Hodgson, was observing the spirited proceedings from some distance away. Cooke spurred swiftly to Major Reno's position, and delivered the orders verbally. The hostiles, he said, were "...about two and a half miles ahead" and "on the jump." Custer's orders to Reno were to charge after them. George Wallace said Reno was told to "go forward as fast as you think proper and charge them wherever you find them!" Custer would bring his column in support behind him. Major Reno's recollection of the orders given by Cooke placed more emphasis upon the village. "General Custer directs you to take as rapid a gait as you think prudent and charge the village afterward and you will be supported by the whole outfit." Major Reno clearly understood what his battalion had been assigned to do. But he was unsure as to what Custer had in mind for his own column.

Custer held back Bouyer and the five Crow scouts. Half Yellow Face advised again that he saw dust and "the Sioux are running away." Custer ordered Half Yellow Face and White Swan to go over the ridge and see for sure what was happening. The two scouts were confused by the sign language, and when they heard the bugle and saw Reno begin to ride, they followed Reno and the 22 Arikara whom Custer had assigned to Reno out of frustration with them.

Custer turned to White-Man-Runs-Him and his companion scouts. Through Mitch Bouyer he told them, "I am through with the scouts. You have brought us to the Sioux." But having now lost most of the scouts, Bouyer called to White-Man-Runs-Him and the others, "Let us go over the ridge and look at the lodges." White-Man-Runs-Him said, "When we reached the ridge we saw the lodges were over in the valley, quite a ways down river, so we went ahead, Custer following. Custer moved slowly and stopped occasionally."

On one stop Custer kneeled to pray. When he got up he shook hands with White-Man-Runs-Him and the other scouts. Then he said, "If we win this battle, you will be the noted men of the Crow Nation.

If I die today, you'll get this land back from the Sioux and stay on it, happy and contented. I am a great chief. I do not know if I will pass through this battle or not. But if I live, I recommend you boys, and you will all be leaders of the Crow. My other scouts are worthless. There will be nothing more good for the Sioux. If they massacre me, they will suffer. If they do not kill me, they will suffer, for they have disobeyed the orders of the Grandfather in Washington. Now let us go."

Soon they climbed the ridge and began to ride parallel to the Little Big Horn River. They now heard the shots of Reno as he engaged the Indians. White-Man-Runs-Him could see the lodges through the timber breaks. He had been right. The number of Sioux was unbelievable. Custer speeded up the column. White-Man-Runs-Him said the smaller Crow ponies could hardly stay up front.

Custer halted the troopers and looked through his glasses. The village seemed deserted. He shouted, "We've got them. We caught them napping! We will finish them off, then go home to our station. Come on!"

On the near side of Medicine Trail Coulee, the scouts found a hilltop where they could see the whole valley. From its head the Coulee sloped down almost a mile to the ford across the Little Big Horn. The troopers readied their weapons.

Custer ordered trumpeter Martin to deliver to Benteen the famous message "...come on – big village – be quick – bring packs. Cooke. P.S. Bring packs." According to White-Man-Runs-Him, the Seventh Cavalry now began the ride down Medicine Trail Coulee. They were about two miles from where Custer's body would later be found. They rode to the Coulee expecting to cross its river.

As they moved down the Coulee, Custer's forces were engaged by a great number of Sioux. Custer turned and moved up a ridge where he dismounted his men. White-Man-Runs-Him and Hairy Moccasin jumped off their horses and provided a protective barrier around Custer. White-Man-Runs-Him observed that the skirmish was very heavy. He and his fellow Crow scouts fired repeatedly at the Sioux.

Bouyer, representing Custer, came up to White-Man-Runs-Him and repeated once again as both he and Custer had said several times before. "You have done your duty. You have led him to the enemy camp and now the thing for you to do is to obey his orders and get away. You go; I am going with the boys." This time, the Crow scouts left. White-Man-Runs-Him often stated afterward, "Had Custer not ordered me to go, the people who visit the Custer Field today would see my name on the monument."

White-Man-Runs-Him, Goes Ahead, and Hairy Moccasin jumped on their horses and rode through the skirmish line toward the bluffs.

From the high point on the bluffs where he could observe what was happening, White-Man-Runs-Him saw Custer, after driving back the first Sioux attack, charge down to the river bank. He saw the Sioux across the river. He saw the Sioux fire. From what he could observe, he concluded that Reno's forces had all been destroyed, and he had little doubt of what was in store for Custer.

While White-Man-Runs-Him did not see what happened to Custer, discussions with the Sioux and Cheyenne several years after the battle caused him to believe that it was at the river where Custer was killed.

As the troopers splashed into the ford, he was told Custer was hit in the chest with a rifle bullet and fell from his horse into the water. He died with the flag on one side of him and Mitch Bouyer on the other. His troopers pulled him from the water and in their panic began to retreat up the little creek that flowed into the Little Big Horn. Custer's body was carried to its final resting place on the hill. The troops, pressured by the Sioux, made their way to the final battle on Monument Hill.

White-Man-Runs-Him, Goes Ahead, and Hairy Moccasin left for the pack train, as ordered by Bouyer. Bouyer had told White-Man-Runs-Him to let the soldiers fight. This was the custom of the plains soldiers — use the scouts to get you there, then release them or use them to drive off the horses, which the Arikara had been ordered to do.

White-Man-Runs-Him, Goes Ahead, and Hairy Moccasin rode toward the pack mules. Captain Benteen's battalion was following in Custer's path about 12 miles back. Benteen first met Sergeant Kanipe, followed shortly by Martin. Martin would be the last white man to see

Custer alive. Benteen pushed down Reno Creek and reached the Little Big Horn just in time to see Reno's men retreating from the valley below where the survivors were gathering on the bluff.

As ordered by Custer, Reno engaged the Indians before Custer. He had crossed the Little Big Horn at Reno Ford. He then led his men on toward the Indian village. Soon the movement of the gathering Indians produced a tremendous dust storm. Unable to see, Reno halted his command and dismounted about 50 yards from the river. As the Indian pressure increased, Reno retreated into a grove of cottonwoods, where he also was able to use the old river bank as a natural barrier. As the warriors worked their way closer to the army, the confusion increased as communication was all but impossible.

After about fifteen minutes, Reno realized he could not hold this position either, so he ordered his men to mount. When Bloody Knife was shot through the head, his brains splashed onto Reno's face, and Reno ordered his men to dismount. After regaining his composure, he ordered his men to mount again. In the confusion, Reno's battalion fled across the river and hurried up the bluffs. Charlie Reynolds was killed as he tried to catch up with the retreating troops.

Reno's command was saved because many Indians withdrew to join their comrades who were engaging Custer. Demoralized and exhausted, Reno's troops expected worse to come.

With the arrival of Benteen's 125 men, Reno pleaded for them to join forces with him. It was about 4:00 P.M. Skirmish lines were formed facing the river, but most of the Indians had withdrawn with only general harassment fire taking place. Reno decided not to try to move the crippled forces until the mule packs caught up.

Reno now wanted to recover Lt. Hodgson's body, which was down by the river. He took about a dozen troopers and went to the river. Indians fired on the party so they were only able to gather some of the dead man's personal possessions. The men filled their canteens and returned to the bluff.

Captain Weir argued with Reno about finding and joining Custer. At first Reno denied the request, but changed his mind in view of regimental honor. Weir, with Company D, mounted and rode to the high bluffs of the north. He advanced about a mile and a half until he came to what is now called Weir's Point. From there, he could see the battlefield, which was obscured by dust and smoke. He could make out Indians riding around shooting at the ground.

Back on Reno Hill, the pack train started to arrive at about 5:00 P.M. It took an hour before all the mules got in. Reno sent Lt. Hare to tell Weir that the rest of the command would follow him as soon as the train was in. He also told him to establish communication with Custer, if possible.

Benteen started off in the direction Weir had taken. The rest of the command followed in a disorganized fashion with many on foot. Six soldiers were needed to carry one wounded man.

Not far from Reno Hill, White-Man-Runs-Him, Goes Ahead, and Hairy Moccasin rode up. They had circled wide from Medicine Trail Coulee. They had noticed Weir and his company in the distance. The scouts told Benteen they were going to cross over the Rosebud and go back up to the Yellowstone River. Unaware of their release by Custer, Benteen now ordered them to stay. White-Man-Runs-Him told of Custer's certain fate, but even Half Yellow Face would not believe him, so he said no more.

Within an hour, the command reached Weir. Almost immediately they were engaged by the Sioux returning from the victory over Custer. White-Man-Runs-Him's horse was shot from under him. As the other members of the command began to come in, Reno ordered a retreat back to the hill. It took them until 7:00 P.M. The Indians pursued, but did not block the troops' movement east.

The outpost, located some 100 feet above the river, was protected as well as possible with boxes and packs at the open end of the Coulee. The last of the troopers had hardly dismounted before the Sioux, fresh from victory and with the benefits of good medicine, had surrounded the command. Even with saddles, which afforded some of the men protection, most men just lay on the ground and hoped for the best. In the three hours before dark, however, 18 were killed and 46 wounded. White-Man-Runs-Him stated that mules were used as breastworks. He helped dig trenches for the ailing troops.

The shooting began to wane as night began to fall. White-Man-Runs-Him, Goes Ahead, and Hairy Moccasin crawled in between several dead mules and waited for the sun to set. In their judgement it was useless to fire in the dark against an unseen enemy. The troops became thirsty. Several details inched their way down the hill to get water. In one case, young Sioux boys threw rocks and mud at the soldiers who came with only buckets. Snipers picked off one trooper and six or seven were wounded.

When the yelling and shooting temporarily stopped, White-Man-Runs-Him spoke to Hairy Moccasin and Goes Ahead. "We were ordered to go. We had better get away from here before the enemy charges in the morning." The scouts spoke of the worry Sits-In-The-Middle-of-the-Land had when they left their people, the danger of leaving the Crow short of warriors should the Sioux attack. Because the scouts feared for their relatives, they returned to the plains Indian philosophy, which stated it was better to retreat from a hopeless situation, in order to live and to fight another day.

As the scouts got up to go, the chief packer saw them and asked where they were headed. White-Man-Runs-Him signaled that they were going for water. The packer then gave each man a canvas-covered flat bottle to fill and bring back. The three scouts left the entrenchment leaving the bottles on the hill.

They had only two horses as they cut across to Reno Creek, following it upstream until they reached a grove of pine trees. Here they ran into four Sioux scouts watching for soldiers. One scout riding a grey horse and leading a mule, lagged far behind the others.

Goes Ahead, in the lead, shot the lone Sioux. When he fell, the reins of the horse were tangled in his legs, forcing the horse to stop in its tracks. Goes Ahead scalped the Sioux as White-Man-Runs-Him and Hairy Moccasin counted coup. White-Man-Runs-Him had been riding double with Hairy Moccasin until the horse wore down. [Pretty Shield believes that White-Man-Runs-Him rode with Goes Ahead.] Then he walked and ran. Unfortunately, he horse was no prize. It was old with a sore back, but it was better than having no horse at all.

In darkness and with rain falling, they reached the Big Horn River, near Hardin, which was swollen as it usually is in June. They could not see the other side, so they waited until morning and swam with their horses to an island. They were cold and hungry, for they had stripped for the fight and left their clothes while they prepared for battle. They had not eaten since the morning before the fighting on the Little Big Horn. White-Man-Runs-Him told Winona Plenty Hoops, "This day was the longest of my life."

It was still raining the next day when White-Man-Runs-Him heard horses. The three scouts who had crossed the river quickly mounted and rode to higher ground. They were afraid the Sioux had discovered them. While on the hill, Crow scouts with Lt. Bradley noticed the three riders on the hill. Bradley had been ordered by Terry to scout the Little Big Horn Valley on the morning of June 26. As the Crow observed the lead Indian scouts, they thought they might be Sioux. Goes Ahead disagreed, saying that he believed them to be Crow. Then, the scouts with Bradley waved blankets.

At first White-Man-Runs-Him, Goes Ahead, and Hairy Moccasin were very cautious. Then they recognized the scouts as No Milk and Plenty Butterflies. They dismounted and quickly built a fire as a signal. Seeing the smoke, Bradley ordered his soldiers to respond with a fire of their own.

The five scouts came together where the river was the narrowest and communicated by sign language. The three Crow scouts told Bradley's Crow that Custer and all of the Blue Soldiers were dead. The Crow with Bradley took the loss of Custer hard, weeping, chanting, mourning, and rocking their bodies. Upon hearing the news, the army soldiers sat in pained silence. Barney Bravo became very excited, then demoralized. No Milk gathered up some extra clothing from the other Crow scouts, which he took to White-Man-Runs-Him, Goes Ahead, and Hairy Moccasin, along with bacon and bread. After they had eaten, they recrossed the river ,where they joined Bradley's forces, who met Terry at noon on the same day. White-Man-Runs-Him had to tell Terry four times about Custer's disaster. Terry remained quiet and seemed to doubt the words he was hearing.

White-Man-Runs-Him also told Terry they had been released by Custer and that he was going home to protect his own people. He further said that their horses were tired and worn out, that they were tired too, and that they needed more clothing and supplies. Barney Bravo, who had been interpreting, added that he had heard Custer and other officers discussing some time ago how the Crow "were only to scout, not fight the Sioux." Terry understood the use of scouts and the constant concern of the military that they fought differently from the soldiers and often got in the military's way. Terry told White-Man-Runs-Him he wanted him and the other scouts to stay, to help lead the other scouts so they might overcome their fears. White-Man-Runs-Him advised Terry if they should find the Sioux camp, then they, too, would all be killed. There were just too many Sioux; their medicine was strong. Terry finally decided to let the three Crow return to their camp; however, he said, "Return quickly."

As White-Man-Runs-Him, Goes Ahead, and Hairy Moccasin left, they were soon joined by a number of Terry's Crows. The return to the Crow camp, now located on Arrow [Pryor] Creek, was uneventful until they were near their village. When the "wolves" of the Crow camp saw the group coming, they mistook them for Sioux. Without waiting to identify the incoming scouts, a war party was quickly raised and charged out of the camp attacking the tired and unsuspecting group with White-Man-Runs-Him. The Custer scouts had no choice but to defend themselves against their own people. Goes Ahead shot and killed one horse, and a second horse was killed by the spraying bullets before the group was recognized.

SOURCES

Chapter VIII

Badhorse, Beverly. "It Is Said That The Chiefs Saw Visions Of The Battle At Foreboding Medicine Rock," *Billings Gazette,* June 23, 1976.
Contains the Cheyenne view of Medicine Rock along with a number of interesting articles on the battle at the Little Big Horn.

Baker, Sue Taylor. "Battle of the Little Big Horn." *Listen.* May, 1977.
Gives information on Curley and his role in the battle. Statement by White-Man-Runs-Him. Also contains information on Chief Spotted Hawk's view of Custer's death as he prepared to cross the river, recorded by his grandson, Les Spotted Hawk of Hardin, Montana.

Billings Gazette (Family Weekly), June 23, 1985.
Information on Custer's drinking and his one time sympathy for the Indian's plight.

Bradley, Lt. James H. *Montana Column.* Norman: University of Oklahoma Press, 1961. Edited by Edgar I. Stewart.
Contains data on the enlistment and a day-by-day account of troop movement.

Dellit, Ursula S. "Notes from Chief Crazy Horse and Max Big Man," June 20, 1935.
Information on the Little Big Horn and the possible death of Custer (mimeographed copy).

Dellit, Ursula S. "Story of the Custer Fight," March 16, 1934.
Contains the story of the Custer fight as told to Dellit by Ben Pease, The story was told to Pease by Ben Spotted Horse (mimeographed copy).

DuBois, Charles. *Custer Mystery.* El Segundo, California: Upton and Son, 1986. *Custer's view on Indian attacks.*

Dustin, Fred. *The Custer Tragedy.* Ann Arbor: Edwards Brothers, Inc., 1939.
Deals with the events of the Little Big Horn and the role of the scouts.

Graham, W. A. *The Custer Myth.* Lincoln and London: University of Nebraska Press, 1953.
Stories of the scouts with various interviewers.

Gray, John S. *Centennial Campaign.* Fort Collins: The Old Army Press, 1976.
Events of the Little Big Horn and information on the scouts.

Libby, O. G. *The Arikara Narrative Of The Campaign Against The Hostile Dakotas June, 1876.* Bismark: North Dakota Historical Collections, 1920.
Information on the Arikara view of the Little Big Horn.

Linderman, Frank B. *Pretty Shield*. Lincoln and London: University of Nebraska, 1932.
Contains Goes Ahead's view about what happened after leaving Reno.

Medicine Crow, Joe. "Interview with Crow Elder," August 31, 1965.
Statement on the death of Custer (mimeographed copy).

Medicine Crow, Joe, Personal Interview.
June 1987–June 1991.
On site inspection of the routes of the Seventh Cavalry, and stories of White-Man-Runs-Him's role in the battle.

Miller, David Humphreys. *Custer's Fall*. Lincoln and London: University of Nebraska, 1957.
Indian view of the Little Big Horn. Has information on the scouts and White-Man-Runs-Him's view of the Arikara.

Plenty Hoops, Winona. Personal Interview.
13 June 1991.
Statements and stories by White-Man-Runs-Him on scouting and the battle.

Sandoz, Mari. *Cheyenne Autumn*. New York: Hastings House, 1953.
Contains information on the possibility of a Custer child.

Schoenberger, Dale. "Custer's Scouts." *Montana The Magazine of Western History*. Spring, 1966.
Custer's scouts.

Stewart, Edgar I. *Custer's Luck*. Norman: University of Oklahoma Press, 1957.
Some information on the weapons of the scouts.

The Tepee Book. *Fiftieth Anniversary of the Custer Battle*. Vol. II., No. VI., June, 1916.
Statements by the scouts and the battle.

Upton, Richard (ed.). *The Indian as a Soldier at Fort Custer Montana 1890–95*. Elsegundo, CA: Upton and Sons, 1983.
Contains information on how the military used scouts.

Vestal, Stanley. *Sitting Bull*. Norman and London: University of Oklahoma Press, 1957.
The Sun Dance of Sitting Bull.

Willert, James. *Little Big Horn Diary*. Whittier: Spectrum Silk Screen, 1977.
Day-by-day account of troop movements.

Wooden Leg. *Wooden Leg*. Lincoln and Norman: University of Nebraska Press, 1931.
A warrior who fought Custer tells of the Cheyenne role in the Little Big Horn and the alcohol found.

IX. A BRIEF REST

After the returning Crow party greeted relatives, nourished themselves, and gathered together fresh clothing, it was time for a meeting with the Council of Chiefs. There the chiefs of the Crow, tribal elders, and a variety of interested parties reviewed the scouting ventures of the Crow enlistees, including the news they had brought of the Custer defeat. White-Man-Runs-Him was especially concerned about the possibility of a Sioux attack on the Crow at the Pryor encampment. He was justified in his concern based upon the numbers alone. At that time the Crow would have been hard-pressed to put more than 1,000 warriors in the field. Even though the Crow had often done well against those who outnumbered them, the strong enemy medicine and sheer force of their numbers certainly seemed to support the Sioux during these times. White-Man-Runs-Him was assured that the Crow scouts reported no Sioux in the immediate area, and yet as White-Man-Runs-Him found out during his return to camp, the Crow were already prepared for whatever might happen.

The Council was intent on finding out all they could about the battle that had taken place. White-Man-Runs-Him spoke of his great liking and admiration for Custer. He pointed out over and over again how this man would have made a great Crow, for even though he had been told of the odds against him, he rode into battle unafraid, prepared to die. For his part, White-Man-Runs-Him argued, as he would throughout his life, that the Sioux and Cheyenne forces numbered between 4000 and 5000 warriors, and quite possibly the number was even greater.

White-Man-Runs-Him was asked by members of the Council what strategy he had advised. While he reported that others disagreed with him, because they believed the Sioux to be on the run, he himself had advised a night attack on the village. A night attack would have given the troopers the advantage of surprise and would have caused the large village to panic and become disorganized. He agreed that as the events of the battle began to unfold, the carelessness of the troops had warned the Sioux of the soldiers' approach. All of those who were involved gave their opinions and answered the questions posed. At one point White-Man-Runs-Him said Custer was "recklessly bold...It was just as if he [Custer] said, 'Reno, you go ahead and let them whip you, and then I will go ahead and they will whip me.'" It was almost as if White-Man-Runs-Him believed that Custer deliberately sacrificed Reno, and then himself. It was clear that the Crow scouts did not understand or agree with the tactics used by the Blue Soldiers.

When the discussions of the Council ended, the scouts seemed to be in agreement that no matter what tactics might have been used, there were just too many desperate Sioux. While White-Man-Runs-Him did not know it at the time, he said years later, "Had Sitting Bull not called a halt to the battle with Reno, they would have died to a man also." During the battle with Reno, Sitting Bull reminded the warriors of his dream and told them:

> Because you have taken the spoils, henceforth you will covet the white man's goods; you will be at his mercy; you will starve at his hands, and the soldiers will crush you... Let them live, they are trying to live. If we kill them all, they will send a bigger army against us.

They were in a sense, trapped, fighting for their land, their women, their children, and a way of life that was being denied them. From the time of this council to the end of his life, White-Man-Runs-Him said, "Had the Terry-Gibbon forces been with Custer that day, then they too would be buried at the Little Big Horn."

When Terry had released the Crow scouts, including White-Man-Runs-Him, Goes Ahead, and Hairy Moccasin, he took his forces onto the battlefield to assess the situation, rescue the survivors, care for the wounded, and bury the dead. The dead were all buried by June 28. They were interned in shallow graves, partly because there were few entrenching tools with the detail, and partly because there was a need to get the wounded to the "Far West" as quickly as possible. The wounded were loaded on the "Far West" on June 30, and then taken to Fort Lincoln.

Almost as soon as the "Far West" left, the Seventh Cavalry was reorganized. Sheridan re-enforced Crook who was ordered to march to the northeast following Rosebud Creek, as Terry and Gibbon moved down from the Yellowstone River. The goal was to detect, capture, and bring into the reservations all the Indians who were roaming off the reservations. If the Indians refused to come in, force was to be used. As in the past, if the Army were to be successful, scouts would be needed. There were none better than the Crow, so Terry ordered Tom LeForge to return to the Crow camp at Pryor to enlist scouts. LeForge was originally with Gibbon's forces. He desired transfer along with White-Man-Runs-Him to Custer's Seventh. It was denied. Later he injured his shoulder and had to be taken to Pease Bottom, at the mouth of the Little Big Horn, where he received medical attention and had his shoulder put in a sling.

LeForge still had three Crow scouts with him. Curley, one of the three, had returned to the "Far West" sometime after the battle. He may have observed the battle from a distance or not witnessed it at all. At any rate, he informed the "Far West" of the Custer defeat. Also with LeForge were two of the original scouts selected by Custer, Half Yellow Face and White Swan, who were with Reno during the Battle at the Little Big Horn. LeForge and his three scouts arrived at the Crow camp not much more than a week after Custer's defeat. They were welcomed and properly received by the Crow.

After learning why LeForge, or "Horse Rider" as he was called, had come, "There was a hubbub of conflicting talk about what should be done in the matter. The subject was discussed in the home lodges that day and night. The next morning, Shot in the Jaw mounted his horse as a crier and rode all through the camps. Everywhere among them he shouted the announcement: 'Horse Rider has something to say in council.'"

The council of chiefs and elders assembled. As a figure of importance, LeForge was seated at the head of the council-lodge. After passing the pipe and a deliberate silence, LeForge was asked "What is your present business with us?" While LeForge answered the question he could hear the noises and words of the people who had gathered outside around the council lodge. Some of the men cheered; others sang war songs; some fired guns into the air. "Conversely, women declared their feelings, 'I shall not permit my husband to go,' or 'my son shall not go to be killed by the Sioux in protection of white soldiers...You have heard what happened to the white soldiers, and the same will happen to our young men if they go to fight the Sioux.'" Other peace-loving people argued. Old women stood here and there chanting of the deaths which were in store for foolish and adventuresome men.

One old man rode among the people and called out, over and over, "I want to get the ear of Horse Rider. He got my ear, as I could hear him urging the warriors to join in the movement." Some of these responded back, "We shall go and when we return, our faces will be painted black," that is, they would kill Sioux in revenge, and the blackened faces would be the token of their victory. A group of women carrying scalps on sticks serenaded the council-lodge near the entrance. Their songs praised the wonderful abilities of Crow warriors. Chief Blackfoot [Sits-In-The-Middle-Of-The-Land] committed himself only by saying, "Yes, they treated our white soldier friends pretty badly and we should not forget this." The council finally arrived at a decision.

A herald was sent among the people to announce: "Young men, we do not send you. But if you want to do so, you may go."

LeForge was successful, and in a short time he had over 50 enlistments. White-Man-Runs-Him enlisted promptly. He remembered Terry's words, to "return quickly." He was rested, his people were still in danger, the white man must be helped, and he still had war honors to complete. It was time to scout once more. LeForge helped promote the new expedition by bringing a dozen or more horses to give to the enlistees. Every individual was promised a saddle-horse, along with pack horses.

LeForge explained to the scouts how they would operate from base camps, making it possible for the men to bring along their women. An additional incentive, which greatly impressed many, was the approach of a steamboat that had arrived at the mouth of Pryor Creek, charged with moving the group to the base camp. The horses were loaded on the lower level of the two-decker, and the passengers, for the most part, rode on the upper deck where they could get a better view.

LeForge reported that it was difficult to keep the boat balanced since the group had the tendency to crowd together in one place, moving from side to side, depending on the significance of the scenery at any given moment.

It must have been quite a sight. The drummers gathered together in the bow and began to beat on their drums, singing songs. The main theme of the war songs that were sung was, "You killed our soldier friends and we shall have revenge." The music, singing, and shouting continued all the way down to the old camp on the north side of the Yellowstone, opposite the mouth of the Big Horn River. As in the past, this military operation would base at the mouth of the Rosebud River and search for the Sioux from that point.

Numerous times White-Man-Runs-Him scouted up the Rosebud, but found nothing other than old tracks and burial scaffolds. After a short time, Crook arrived and White-Man-Runs-Him was transferred to his command. With Crook, he led the way up the Rosebud, across the divide, and into the valley of the Tongue. Conditions were extremely difficult. The water was heavy with alkali, and many of Crook's men had severe stomach problems.

The unit continued its movement to the east until they came to the Powder River, where camp was made primarily to rest the overtired men and horses. There was, however, no rest for White-Man-Runs-Him. His legend of having traveled on foot for long distances under Gibbon and Custer had preceded him. He was regarded as someone who could meet the tests of the trail and still succeed. While the others rested, he, along with Buffalo Bill Cody, a scout with Crook, and several others, were asked to take a message to General Miles, who was camped on the Yellowstone.

The 12 mile journey revealed many freshly-made Sioux tracks. As the party reached the Yellowstone River, White-Man-Runs-Him discovered thousands of bushels of corn that appeared to have been scattered along the bank of the river. The corn had been brought up by steamers and stacked on the river bank for the soldiers operating in the area. The Sioux had discovered the catche, cut open the canvas sacks and taken them, leaving the corn for the forces of nature to deal with.

When White-Man-Runs-Him found General Miles, he delivered the message that Miles should hold his place because Crook was on his way. Since Crook was soon to arrive, White-Man-Runs-Him did not make the return trip, but rather refreshed himself with a meal and some much needed sleep. In view of the whiskey controversy of the Custer expedition, an interesting incident took place at Miles camp. A flatboat loaded with liquor arrived, and its manager made a significant amount of money selling to the thirsty soldiers on the war front. Barney Bravo became wild with intoxication. His friends, the Crow, who refrained from the "fire water" themselves, tied him up and put him in one of the tents to sleep it off.

When Crook arrived, the officers had a big conference. In short, they decided the scouts were correct in reporting that the Sioux had broken into smaller bands, probably because there wasn't enough food available for large numbers. Sitting Bull would be leaving for Canada with his group, and Crazy Horse had moved into the Big Horn Mountains. Many of those who were gathered together at the Little Big Horn had returned to their reservations, where the policy of the government was to disarm and settle them. The officers agreed they would end the large campaign concept for the time being.

Miles was to go up Powder River and establish a permanent base while Gibbon would return to Fort Ellis and then to Fort Shaw. Terry would take his men and leave for Fort Lincoln. White-Man-Runs-Him, along with the other Crow, was informed they were officially released and would be discharged in due form. With this news, the Crow returned to the camp on the Rosebud River, gathered together their women and possessions, and slowly started to move toward Fort Ellis. They were given no food before they left, making it necessary to hunt and eat those things nature had long provided for them. After crossing to the south side of the Yellowstone, they waited for Gibbon's column, and then followed them on into Fort Ellis. At Fort Ellis, on September 30, 1876, White-Man-Runs-Him was formally discharged as a private.

After receiving their pay, White-Man-Runs-Him and most of the other scouts traveled on to Bozeman. In Bozeman they found it easy to spend their money, purchasing all kinds of provisions, including blankets, tobacco, calico, and ammunition. Some of the Crow had very little money left by the time they got to Bozeman because they had purchased "racing horses" before they left Fort Ellis. These Crow were exposed for the first time to the racing of horses, white man's style, when they observed the events involving "racers" from Bozeman and the Gallatin Valley. Upon their return to Pryor, horse racing became an interest of the former scouts, as the new horses were tested against the best ponies of the Crow nation.

White-Man-Runs-Him began to settle back into the Crow lifestyle, even taking himself a wife, when a Captain Hargus and some members of the Fifth Infantry came to visit the Crow at Absarokee. With the approval of the Council of Chiefs, the old Agency near Livingston, called Fort Parker, had been moved in 1875 to the Rosebud Creek, about two miles from its confluence with the Stillwater River. About a half-dozen families were farming, but most of the Crow went to the Big Horn country in the spring to hunt buffalo and returned in midsummer to dress hides. They stayed at Absarokee until autumn, and then left to again hunt buffalo in the fall. In early January they returned to the Agency.

Representing General Miles and the Fifth Infantry, Captain Hargus came to Absarakee to enlist the help of the Crow. White-Man-Runs-Him was ready to serve with his old friends Tom LeForge and General Miles. Even though White-Man-Runs-Him was looking forward to participating in tribal affairs, the call to scout came again. Miles had asked for the best scouts, and while volunteers were not hard to get, it was expected that White-Man-Runs-Him would go. Besides the call of a new adventure, White-Man-Runs-Him had been treated well by the whites in the past. He could use the money and Miles promised that wives and families would again be welcome. Two days after Captain Hargus had come, White-Man-Runs-Him headed for Fort Keogh, named after Captain Keogh who had been killed with Custer. The new fort was located near the mouth of the Tongue River on the south side of the Yellowstone.

Almost as soon as White-Man-Runs-Him became familiar with the fort, his first mission began. A band of Cheyenne had been seen to the east. Major Brisbin, the cavalry commander, with the Crow scouts in the lead, gave chase. They crossed the Powder River, then followed the trails leading to the Black Hills. They pushed on to the Heart River, where they met up with Colonel Gibson. After the two military leaders conferred, it was decided that if there had been any

White-Man-Runs-Him.(Courtesy of the National Battlefield Archives, Crow Agency, Montana.)

133

Cheyenne in the vicinity, they had avoided the troops, so the order was given to return to the fort. The march home proved to be a difficult one. The unit had used almost all of its food supplies, and the area seemed to be devoid of big game. Some mules were killed and prepared for food. White-Man-Runs-Him said that the Crow would not eat mule as long as there were prairie dogs in great abundance.

Fuel was also in short supply. There was no wood and without buffalo in the area, there were no chips to burn. Fires were made from grass that had been rubbed down with bacon grease to increase the heat level. One of the few successful hunts during this venture belonged to White-Man-Runs-Him, who shot a fawn as he was leading the troops down the Powder River. LeForge recalled how the deer was shared with friends, and even though the meat was gone after one meal, it certainly raised spirits.

Several days later while out on a scouting mission to find food, White-Man-Runs-Him discovered the scattered remains of a pack train which was supposed to have met the troops some time earlier, but was never was able to find them. White-Man-Runs-Him raced his pony back to the command as quickly as he could and requested help to bring in the cargo left by the packers. Returning with several troopers, they packed up hardtack, bacon, and other provisions lying on the trail. Needless to say, White-Man-Runs-Him saw his prestige increase among the grateful troopers and officers.

In terms of bringing in the Cheyenne, the trip was without success. No Indians were sighted, nor were any fresh trails discovered. It had been a difficult journey for White-Man-Runs-Him's wife, but she made no complaints during the trying trek. Everyone was glad to reach the confines of Fort Keogh. A banquet was held with the celebration continuing into the early morning. For the next several weeks both troopers and scouts relaxed, enjoying their free time after the tiring venture to capture the nonexistent Cheyenne. Then one day a group of Crow scouts, including White-Man-Runs-Him, decided to go hunting. While in the hills, they noticed a band of Sioux moving through a ravine. The Crow did not know that the Sioux were coming in as representatives from a band up on the Power River to discuss possible surrender with General Miles. The Crow decided this was an opportunity to do something important for the army. After discussing the matter briefly, they attacked the incoming Sioux , killing five and driving off the others. They picked up the dead, placed them on their ponies and returned to the fort. When they found out the Sioux were coming in under a white flag, the Crow were extremely embarrassed. They were shamed, for according to custom, "They were now considered outlaws who could be continually hunted until their death." White-Man-Runs-Him was embarrassed and heartbroken. He told his friends that he had always respected the flag of truce. "The Sioux carried no flag, and the Crow had not been informed of their coming in. Still the officers would be upset."

All of the Crow scouts now went into Council trying to decide what to do. Two nights later, most of the scouts including White-Man-Runs-Him decided to leave. White-Man-Runs-Him left with his wife because he was concerned for her safety should the Sioux decide to seek revenge. The group packed and headed up the Yellowstone River, leaving only Half Yellow Face and Long Ago Bear as post scouts. Long Ago Bear's wife, Emma Chein, and their two daughters, Mary and Elizabeth, also remained. Emma, Joe Medicine Crow's great grandmother, had been acting as interpreter for the scouts. One day while exploring the site where the Sioux had been killed, Mary and Elizabeth found a telescope. Inside the telescope the girls discovered a roll of paper money. Perhaps the telescope and the contents came from the Little Big Horn.

In the spring of 1877, Lt. Doane, of the Second Cavalry, was commissioned to set up a new post on the Big Horn to be called Fort Custer. The area selected for the fort was located on a bench near the junction of the Little Big Horn and Big Horn Rivers, not more than 15 miles down the valley from where the so called "Last Stand" took place. More Crow were needed to help protect the workers who were to construct the fort. Since the incident with the Sioux had been forgotten, White-Man-Runs-Him consented to be a part of the scouts. In June, it was announced that the newly recruited I. Company, Seventh Cavalry, under Captain Henry J. Nowlan was dispatched from the mouth of the Tongue River to gather up the remains of officers and rebury the soldiers who had fallen in 1876 at the Little Big Horn. Lt. Hugh Scott, later Major General Scott, along with Colonel Mike Sheridan were to accompany Nowlan and his reburial detail. Since they needed scouts, they stopped on the way to enlist the Crow. They were especially interested in the scouts who had participated in the battle of Little Big Horn. It was believed that White-Man-Runs-Him, Hairy Moccasin, White Swan, Half Yellow Face, Goes Ahead, and Curley could add to the historical explanation of the fight, as well as help read the terrain, and perhaps discover missing bodies.

The detail arrived at the site on June 25, 1877, one year after the battle had taken place. White-Man-Runs-Him had been back to the battlefield on several occasions prior to his return with the burial details. He noted the amazement of the burial party at the length of the grass, which was as high as the bellies of the horses. There were flowers growing everywhere and the area looked different than it had a year ago when the warriors of the Sioux and Cheyenne had inflicted a terrible defeat on the white soldiers. The great encampment of one year earlier still had a number of lodge poles standing. Many hides were noticeable on the ground, and a variety of other material possessions were still in place where they had been left. The Crow had not camped near the Little Big Horn since the great fight, for they said it "smelled of death for a year after the battle."

White-Man-Runs-Him told Winona Plenty Hoops, "It was not as they said." He was referring to the official reports of Nolan, Godfrey, and Sheridan. White-Man-Runs-Him agreed with LeForge, who said that there were many skulls and bones exposed, some totally and others only partially. The soil was powdery and there were few rocks with which they could have covered the graves. Many soldiers had only been covered with dirt. Most who were buried in graves in 1876 had been placed in pits less than 20 inches in depth.

White-Man-Runs-Him said the wolves and coyotes were at work from the first, often digging up the bodies and dragging them and the bones for some distance from the graves, which may or may not have represented the places where the men actually fell or were found. While a search was conducted on the field for all of the remains in 1877, White-Man-Runs-Him has since been proven correct when he stated that "There were bones and men who were not found...They put the markers where they wanted." He also thought that little care was taken to rebury the enlisted men whose bones were collected in piles where they lay and placed in graves as shallow as the originals. The first hard rains would again uncover them.

The real purpose of the burial details in 1877 was to recover the bones of the officers, then send them on the steamboat "Fletcher" to Fort Lincoln, and from there to various destinations for final burial. The remains of Custer, Keogh, Tom Custer, Yates, Cooke, Smith, Reily, Hodgson, and Dr. DeWolf, were gathered and identified. White-Man-Runs-Him did not agree that great care was taken to properly identify each man. White-Man-Runs-Him noted that the bones of some were mixed with the bones of others. Elizabeth Custer had heard of such stories and had to be assured several times that the General's bones were actually his and were all in place. Both White-Man-Runs-Him and Tom LeForge watched as General Custer's remains were gathered together. About all that remained "was a thigh bone and the skull attached to part of the trunk...The location of the bodies, their prior burial, and their state of existence was not as they said."

SOURCES

Chapter IX

Dixon, Joseph K. *The Vanishing Race.* New York: Popular Library, 1923.
Comments on the battle from White-Man-Runs-Him.

Graham, W. A. *The Custer Myth.* Lincoln and London: University of Nebraska Press, 1953.
Contains General Hugh Scott's interview with White-Man-Runs-Him, and burial of the dead compiled by Fred Dustin including Col. Sheridan's report, General Godfrey's description, and Trumpeter Mulford's viewpoint.

LeForge, Thomas. *Memoirs of a White Crow Indian.* Lincoln and London: University of Nebraska, 1974.
Scouting and burial.

Medicine Crow, Joseph. Letter. 6 September 1991.
White-Man-Runs-Him's life after the battle.

Medicine Crow, Joseph. Personal interview.
14 June 1991.
White-Man-Runs-Him's life after the battle.

Plenty Hoops, Winona. Personal interview.
13 June 1991.
Statements of White-Man-Runs-Him.

Vestal, Stanley. *Sitting Bull.* Norman and London: University of Oklahoma Press, 1932.
The role of Sitting Bull.

X. LIFE AFTER THE WARS

When the Crow scouts were again called upon to help the United States Army subdue the Nez Perce, White-Man-Runs-Him was not among those who decided to enlist. Some have suggested that he decided not to go because he believed he was not in good favor with the military since the mistaken killing of the Sioux while he was with General Miles. This does not seem likely, however, since he had been invited on the reburial detail at the battlefield without incident. There is little doubt that he was still extremely loyal to the American flag and would be until the day he died.

A better explanation for his lack of interest in enlisting against the Nez Perez appears to be his recognition that the Indian way of life was ending. White-Man-Runs-Him had by then spent enough time with the white man to recognize things would never be the same. Perhaps he realized that the struggle of the Nez Perce represented a final blow to native peoples, regardless of loyalties past or present. White-Man-Runs-Him was also familiar with the Nez Perce. They had been on good terms with the Crow and had even sought Crow aid in this struggle for their land. In fact the Nez Perce were taken aback when the Crow refused to guarantee them safe passage across Crow land. In any case, White-Man-Runs-Him was not with the Crow who helped bring Chief Joseph down in the Bear Paw Mountains in 1877.

According to Indian Agent Keller, there were 3300 Crow in 1879. While the whites still were trying to make farmers out of the Crow, only 20 acres of land were under plow. A handful had learned to read, and about 100 or so were starting to wear white man's clothing. The great majority of Crow, including White-Man-Runs-Him continued to practice the old ways as best they could. They remained nomadic, moving camp frequently, and functioning in increasingly smaller bands of about 30 members.

By 1881, White-Man-Runs-Him had joined the Buffalo Chapter of the Tobacco Society. The tobacco ceremony had originally been conveyed to No Vitals during the migration period. At that time, No Vitals had been told that when men had been created, each tribe was given special powers. "He Who Made All Things" instructed that tobacco was a most sacred power, one that could bestow great blessings on an individual or a people. There was a proper way to plant the seed: incense was to be used, songs sung, and ceremonies performed. Then the plant had to be picked in the accepted way, the harvesters not touching it with bare skin for fear of having sores cover their bodies.

In earlier times there had been only a few chapters of the Tobacco Society; however, as time went on, new chapters were created through the powerful visions of certain individuals. White-Man-Runs-Him was adopted into the Buffalo Chapter by Big-Shoulder-Blade, the founder. Big-Shoulder-Blade made a headpiece for White-Man-Runs-Him consisting of buffalo horns with a buffalo tail attached. Chapter members also made martingales from the tails of buffalo for their horses, with bells attached to the tails. When Big-Shoulder-Blade died, White-Man-Runs-Him was honored by being selected as the painter of the sacred symbols for the Buffalo Chapter.

White-Man-Runs-Him was not yet directly involved in tribal politics, but he was greatly concerned by the events of the 1880s. In 1879, the United States Government called for a delegation of Crow to come to Washington to discuss the acquisition of more Crow land. At first the Crow resisted, sending word to Washington that they did not wish to part with any more land, and wouldn't, unless forced to. The Crow, however, went to Washington in 1880, and came home having relinquished 1,500,000 acres of land. In 1881 a tract of 400 feet of right-of-way was lost to the Northern Pacific for a railway along the Yellowstone.

By 1905, the reservation had been reduced by 3 million acres. The Crow received less than five cents per acre for their land, and the reservation was now about eight percent of its original size. The enemies of the Crow, who were still bitter because the Crow had not joined in the conflict with the whites, looked on with great satisfaction as the Crow territory was reduced in size.

In April, 1884, the Crow Agency was moved for the last time to its present location on the banks of the Little Big Horn River. By this

White-Man-Runs-Him wearing the headgear given him by Big-Shoulder-Blade.

time, it was clear to White-Man-Runs-Him it would be almost impossible to win full chieftainship. While raids would continue for several more years among the tribes of the area, White-Man-Runs-Him saw values and traditions changing; traditional times were coming to an end, and the ways of the warrior were over.

It was the policy of the government to confine the Crow more and more to the reservation and to "civilize" them. In the process, the Council of Chiefs, as it had been known, was dissolved. The government desired to deal with just one chief. In the past, prestige and leadership had been won by gaining war honors and by action. It now became difficult to find a single leader. Crow men were at a loss, because the their number-one goal was no longer possible to achieve. To the Crow male, it was undignified to participate in tribal decision-making without the proper warrior society's credentials. Thus, the result was political disorganization. The Indian Agent now took over the tribal decision-making process in "Kingly" fashion.

Times were tough for White-Man-Runs-Him. He took interest in the Dawes Act of 1887, which provided for the division of tribal lands among individual members. While the act did not benefit White-Man-Runs-Him until 1901, he survived through hunting and living off the land. As a result of the division of Crow tribal property, White-Man-Runs-Him was able to claim 320 acres of land divided into eight 40-acre lots. While he never gave up the closeness he felt for nature and continued to hunt, the private acreage allowed him to raise some horses that he later sold to the army and to local ranchers. Montana became the 41st state in the Union in 1889. It was time to settle down. He built his home on one of the plots of land he acquired in what is still known as the "Valley of the Chiefs." The beautiful valley, named because of the great number of chiefs who settled there, is located at the junction of Lodge Grass Creek and the Little Big Horn River, moving upstream on or close to Lodge Grass Creek near the present-day town of Lodge Grass.

In 1903, Reverend W. A. Petzoldt and his wife Anna came to the Crow for the purpose of establishing a Baptist Mission and school. The Petzoldts described the reservation at that time as having no roads, only wagon tracks, no fences, and little plowed land. Many

Crow were still living in tepees, with a few scattered homes, many of which were made from the material confiscated from old Fort Custer.

White-Man-Runs-Him took to the Petzoldts from their first meeting, and the couple reciprocated. The Crow had been upset for some time by the concept of boarding schools that took children away from their parents and homes for the purpose of education. White-Man-Runs-Him became interested in the boarding school problem because he had children of his own, and it was expected that they would go to the school. His interest was further stimulated because of an incident in the life of his good friend, Chief Spotted Horse, and his daughter Clara, who had been attending the school.

According to Winona Plenty Hoops, her mother Clara was in school when she and quite a number of students became ill. A number of children died of the illness, and Spotted Horse became very concerned. He went to the school intent on bringing his daughter home, where he believed she would recover in the safety of her own home and the good care of her own mother. When Spotted Horse got to the agency, he told the authorities he wanted to take his daughter home. The officials denied his request, telling Spotted Horse she could not leave. Spotted Horse told the school officials this was a "great unfairness." After further discussion, Spotted Horse became angry. He finally took out his hunting knife, which he always carried. The school authorities called for help and several men quickly appeared. Spotted Horse repeated his demand to take his daughter, then told everyone in the room, "I wish to do no one harm...", but "no one should be so foolish as to try and stop me." He then picked up Clara and returned home as the officials watched. The child quickly recovered, as Spotted Horse had predicted.

In an attempt to remedy the boarding school situation, Spotted Horse requested a meeting with the Council of Chiefs. White-Man-Runs-Him, Medicine Crow, and Yellowtail were among the 30 chiefs who met with the Petzoldts to discuss their concerns. For his part, White-Man-Runs-Him argued as did others who spoke to the Council of Chiefs that represented the six Crow Districts: "Boarding schools are not good for the Crow. They take our children when they are four years old; they lock them up and we can't see them but once in six months. I don't like this. Why can't we have our own school during the day, so our children can sleep at home during the night?"

As a result of the discussions, the Petzoldts worked with the chiefs and the Crow people to establish the first Indian day school in the nation. White-Man-Runs-Him never forgot the Petzoldts and their help and understanding in establishing the day school.

As was custom among the Crow, White-Man-Runs-Him had not sought a wife until after he acquired honors in war. He was married for the first time and divorced prior to the Custer fight. Among the Crow, when marriage was considered, it was the custom to present horses to the brother or brothers of the prospective bride. Another tradition sometimes followed was to approach the maiden directly, presenting her with a gift, usually a top-notch pony. If the man was acceptable, then the couple agreed to elope at a predetermined time. Often they would live for some time with the husband's parents, where the wife would learn from the mother-in-law while she worked for the family. Gifts were usually presented to the new bride by her husband's parents.

In earlier times, a wife who had committed adultery could be beaten and perhaps even have her body slashed by her husband. Quite often a Crow male would "throw away" a wife, sometimes even giving away horses in the "throw away." The releasing of a wife could result from a problem in the marriage between the couple or between their in-laws. During the Crow "hot dance," anyone wishing to throw away a wife could do so during the singing of a special song. In the case of divorce, young children usually went with the mother who had been given up. While not frequently done, there are instances in Crow culture where the wife threw away her husband.

In his book *The North American Indian*, Curtis reported that White-Man-Runs-Him had been married seven times. "Of his seven wives he gave up six 'good ones,' that is, those who had born him children: to discard such wives was an indication of a strong heart." Whether or not White-Man-Runs-Him was married seven times can not be supported. Only his last and most successful marriage was officially recorded. All previous marriages and divorces were in his words, "by Indian custom," and the dates are subject to debate and much speculation.

His first wife was a Crow woman named Fat Snake. A son named Bull-On-The-Other-Side-of-The-Hill stayed with his mother by custom, and no father-son relationship, as is the custom today, developed between them.

It is generally agreed his second marriage was to a Flathead woman and that a daughter was born of the marriage. The name of the wife and the daughter have been lost to the family, and the records are unclear. Sometime after this divorce, he traveled with relatives to North Dakota to visit relations there. There, he allegedly met a Hidatsa woman, married, and had a daughter named Sweet Cherry or Cherries.

His fourth wife was named Horse. Three children were born from this relationship. Tillie was born in 1888, Blake in 1892, and John in 1893. Horse was also given away at a public ceremony by White-Man-Runs-Him. Tradition holds that she had been having an affair with Ben Spotted Horse and the embarrassment was so great that White-Man-Runs-Him specifically gave her to Spotted Horse around 1897. Spotted Horse accepted her and they were married. White-Man-Runs-Him did not raise his own children and Tillie and Blake attended the boarding school at Crow Agency. Tillie married at a young age and Blake was adopted by his maternal aunt, Mrs. Packs the Hat shortly after White-Man-Runs-Him's divorce. His son John lived with his grandfather, Bull-Chief. John entered the boarding school and upon graduation married Amy Yellowtail.

In 1902, White-Man-Runs-Him was called to the home of his long-time friend, Chief Spotted Horse, who recently had an accident while breaking a horse. The horse had fallen over backward and then rolled over on him, causing serious internal injuries. When White-Man-Runs-Him entered the Spotted Horse home, another man was also there. Spotted Horse called them together and told them that he had asked his wife, Pretty Medicine Pipe to prepare a fine meal for them. After the meal was eaten, Spotted Horse told his wife and the two men that at first he thought he would soon get better, but as time went on, the hurt inside was getting worse. He conveyed to the group that he would soon die. Then he told the two men with Pretty Medicine Pipe listening: "You are my best friends, I have three children; they need a father to love and raise them. You are good men.

I want you two to talk it over and decide. I want one of you to marry my wife."

Spotted Horse then told his wife not to refuse the request of marriage from either man. He further suggested she should marry as soon as convenient and not wait the customary one year for mourning. Soon after the request was made by Spotted Horse, the other man at the meeting died. Spotted Horse followed him in death shortly thereafter. Being true to his friend, White-Man-Runs-Him honored his request and married Pretty Medicine Pipe in a ceremony performed by Mr. Burgess at Crow Agency, Montana, on October 15, 1904.

Pretty Medicine Pipe's father was the half-breed son of a trapper. She had been married once before to Chief Old Crow, who she had accompanied to Washington with the delegation of 1872. According to Winona Plenty Hoops, White-Man-Runs-Him and Pretty Medicine Pipe had a very positive relationship, based on "love and respect".

White-Man-Runs-Him adopted the Spotted Horse children. Winona Plenty Hoops remembers he never raised his voice in anger and he kept everything in perspective around the home. "He was a good father and treated his family with generosity." White-Man-Runs-Him and Pretty Medicine Pipe later adopted and helped raise several grandchildren. The discipline in the home was, for the most part, handled by Pretty Medicine Pipe, for White-Man-Runs-Him remained "good-natured."

SOURCES

Chapter X

"Bureau of Indian Affairs Records." Crow Agency, Montana. Records of marriages.

"Crow Agency allotment records." National Archives Pacific-Northwest Region.
White-Man-Runs-Him's allotment.

Curtis, Edward S. *The North American Indian.* Vol. III. New York: Johnson Reprint Corporation, 1908.
Contains information on White-Man-Runs-Him and the Buffalo Chapter.

Hardin Tribune-Herald, Hardin, Montana, August 14, 1958.
Contains an article on the death of Mrs. W. A. Petzoldt and the history of the Petzoldts' work in Lodge Grass.

Hoxie, Frederick E. "Building A Future On The Past: Crow Indian Leadership in an Era of Division and Reunion." *National Anthropological Archives,* Bureau of Ethnology Collection.
Contains information on Agent Keller's description of the reservation.

Marquis, Arnold. *A Guide to American Indians.* Norman: University of Oklahoma Press, 1978.
Information on Crow history and the decrease in the size of the Crow reservation.

Medicine Crow. Personal interview.
16-17 June1991.
White-Man-Runs-Him's role in the creation of the day school and his marriage to Pretty Medicine Pipe.

Plenty Hoops, Winona. Personal interview.
13 June1991.
Stories about White-Man-Runs-Him.

XI. THE WANAMAKER MEMORIAL

On February 7, 1913, Winfield Scott, now Superintendent of the Crow Agency, received a telegram followed by a letter from F. H. Abbott, Acting Commissioner of Indian Affairs. In essence, the letter and telegram read that if the tribal council should approve the payment of expenses from tribal funds, the Bureau would like White-Man-Runs-Him, Plenty Coups, Medicine Crow, and Frank Shively as interpreter, to come to Washington to attend and participate in the laying of the cornerstone to the Wanamaker monument to the American Indian. Abbott emphasized no one should be selected who couldn't "bring full Indian costume, including war bonnets, blankets, leggings, moccasins, etc."

The Crow Council was called into session, and after much discussion, asked Scott to return a telegram stating that they insisted upon selecting their own people and would like to add two more.

On February 10, the Crow Council met and decided that while the delegation was participating in the dedication ceremony in New York, they might as well meet with Abbott and discuss the concerns of the Crow Nation.

Thus, the Crow delegation made its way to Washington by rail. First, they would participate in the dedication of the National Memorial, then they would make a quick tour of Philadelphia and, upon their return to Washington, they would meet with Abbott and discuss the issues of concern of their people.

White-Man-Runs-Him and the Crow delegation hardly made it to Washington, before they were boarded on a train speeding for New York's Pennsylvania Station. They arrived at 4:45 P.M., February 22, 1913, along with 29 other chiefs and important leaders from the west. On February 23, the *New York Times* reported:

> Chiefs of Dying Race Here For Honors. Noted Red Men arrive
> from the West to attend the unveiling of a statue to their ancestors.

To Greet White Father men who fought Custer and Miles stalk proudly through crowds on the way to their hotel.

White-Man-Runs-Him and his fellow delegates were greeted by George and Mrs. Bird-Grinnell, authors, and a variety of reporters and photographers. "The Indian dignitaries did not blink as the flashes shot from the cameras." White-Man-Runs-Him was dressed in one of his three famous coats of leather and fur. Others wore eagle feathers and assorted head and neck bands. They were dressed for the most part in white man's clothing. The Indian clothing they would wear for the Wanamaker ceremony was provided for them, even though they had been requested to bring their own.

As the crowd of interested people grew, the delegation discovered they were to have been met by Major James McLauglin, Government Inspector of Reservations and an old friend of many Indians. McLaughlin had been delayed and when the delegation found out they were to be housed in the Mills Seventh Avenue Hotel, they rebelled, as they wanted to stay with McLaughlin, who was staying in the Herald Square Hotel.

The delegation moved to the Herald Square, where the clerks scrambled but were unable to accommodate them. They then moved back to the Mills Hotel, but would not consent to stay in separate rooms. With the crowds increasing, they went back to the Herald and after some period of waiting, moved down Sixth Avenue to the Cosmopolitan Hotel, where most went to bed early. White-Man-Runs-Him and several others explored Broadway.

It is interesting to note that many newspapers in the east were mistaken when they reported that "White-Man-Runs-Him of the Crows, still bears the name they gave him for the scout service he did for Custer when he led the General's men into the Valley of the Little Big Horn."

White-Man-Runs-Him and his fellow delegates were up early the next day. They ate breakfast and left the Cosmopolitan Hotel (Chambers and West Broadway) and boarded the army steamboat, the "General Johnson" at 10:00 A.M. The "General Johnson" left the pier at East Twenty Fourth Street to carry the delegation to Fort Wadsworth. At Fort Wadsworth they were to meet many noted men including

Secretary Stimson, Admirals Dewey and Osterhaus, General Woods and Barry and a number of senators and house members, along with a multitude of dignitaries.

At last the time had come to honor the American Indian. This was to be the world's first monument to an entire race. Dr. Joseph Kossuth Dixon, author of *The Vanishing Race*, was present, and so was Rodman Wanamaker, the brainchild behind the monument and the financial backer.

Rodman Wanamaker was the son of John Wanamaker. Both worked together with John's brother Thomas, to build a gigantic and successful merchandising business in both Philadelphia and New York. The Wanamakers were literally involved in all aspects of American life, including politics, business, aviation, industry, foreign policy, transportation, religion, and much more. They traveled extensively throughout the United States and the world and their philanthropy was extensive.

Rodman's interest in Indians was stimulated by his father, and he made it his goal to bring about Indian citizenship. He hoped to tell the Indians' story through promotional ideas designed to record Indian culture in a native setting. He also attempted to foster Indian allegiance and friendship toward the United States government.

As a result, he financed three expeditions into the west. In 1908, he led an educational expedition to the Crow Reservation in Montana to make a movie of Hiawatha. It was here he probably first met and befriended White-Man-Runs-Him.

In 1909, Wanamaker sponsored a second expedition called the "Last Great Indian Council" and recorded in motion pictures. He also used an all Indian cast and filmed the reenactment of the "Battle of the Little Big Horn." Whether White-Man-Runs-Him participated in the film is uncertain; however, the chances are good that he did. The movies were first shown to President Taft, his cabinet, the State Department, both Houses of Congress, and the Federal Judiciary. As a result of the expedition's research, a primer, or text, called the *Indian Primer* was developed and issued to 225,000 private and public schools.

It was sometime prior to his second expedition that Wanamaker got the idea for a National Memorial to the American Indian. His suggestion was made in the following letter to President Taft on May 12, 1909:

Dear Mr. President:

I desire to have the honor to propose to you that if the sentiment of the American people is such, I would like to have your cooperation, with permission and grants from Congress, in placing on Lafayette Island, in the New York harbor, a statue of the North American Indian — the first inhabitant and Citizen of this continent and the accepted symbol of the United States.

This statue, heroic in size, would stand at the eastern gateway of our country, with outstretched arms in welcome, by day or night, if it was deemed advisable to serve as a harbor light, to all those coming to this land of liberty and freedom, recognizing also the welcome which the Red Man gave to the White Man when our forefathers first came to these shores.

I therefore respectfully request that you lay before your committees this matter for presentation to Congress, and beg of you to ask the cooperation of your bodies, as well as of the American people who desire to participate in this work of patriotism, and would request that privilege of Congress would be given to commence the work immediately.

I beg to remain with great respect,

Rodman Wanamaker

During the evening of May 12, the same day he sent the letter to the President, Rodman Wanamaker hosted a banquet in honor of Buffalo Bill Cody. In attendance were such dignitaries as Bill Cody, Pawnee Bill, Generals Nelson Miles and Leonard Wood, Frederic Remington, and Homer Davenport.

Most of the speakers at Sherrys, New York, spoke on behalf of the Wanamaker Memorial. Buffalo Bill Cody gave the following speech:

The Indian — I have known him since I was a baby; since I was old enough to know anything; I have met him in councils; I have met him on the war path, and I must say that I have never found him dishonorable in peace or war. Many unthinking people say, 'Why do the Indians go to war and why are they so cruel in mutilating the

At Wanamaker's store, Philadelphia. White-Man-Runs-Him seated third from left.
(Photo courtesy Pennsylvania Historical Society.)

White-Man-Runs-Him was selected to be the model for the Memorial to the American
Indian to be built in the New York Harbor.

victims whom they kill?' I do not know, but I do know that they have been driven from the Pacific Ocean to the Atlantic and back and forth again, until they are as wanderers upon the face of the land they once owned. They gave them a little strip of land here on the Atlantic coast and told them they would be glad to have the whites with them.

More whites came and the Indians gave them still more land. Finally so many whites came that they told the Indians they must move west of the Alleghanies and then they would not be bothered any more. But how long did this last? Soon, the pioneers, like Daniel Boone and many others, came to the Alleghanies and the Indians had to move again.

They said, "Let them go west of the Mississippi River, a country only fit for Indians, coyotes, and rattlesnakes." Fifty years ago our ablest diplomats and statesmen said the land west of the Mississippi and especially around the Mississippi River, was fit for nothing else but Indians and wild animals. We all know that country is getting to be the best part of America, and the land where the coyote and the buffalo and the Indians roamed now blossoms and blooms as a rose.

The Indian thought he could remain there forever, but he had to go still farther to the Black Hills. The white man followed him there, against the will of the United States Government, and took that land from the Indians, given to them by a treaty made for the United States Government by the Interior Department. As soon as gold was discovered here, Mr. Indian had to walk out, and they were driven from that home where they had buried their fathers and mothers.

It is a great satisfaction to me to feel – I do not know it, I have only got that little feeling – that there is a man here tonight who has been sending these expensive expeditions into the West for the purpose of gathering the history of the Indians and becoming familiar with them, and his heart seems to be in that direction. Why is he doing it unless he intends doing something more to perpetuate the memory of the Indian? I have got that little feeling that he intends to build a monument here in New York Harbor as large as the Goddess of Liberty, with an Indian on top showing him as he was when the whites first visited America, with his hands extended welcoming every one to this shore.

Major-General Nelson A. Miles also spoke that evening:

Our relations with the Indians as a race have been no credit to us. The early explorers kidnapped them on the coast and carried them to distant lands, there to exhibit them; they were sold into slavery in Massachusetts, Connecticut, Rhode Island, New York, Delaware, Virginia and the Carolinas; they were hunted with dogs in Connecticut, and at one time the assembly at New Haven appropriated $250.00 for the purchase and maintenance of a pack of hounds to hunt the Indians. Those acts caused a bitter feeling among the two races, causing the Indian to distrust the whites, and war soon followed, incited by a spirit of revenge, which lasted for two hundred years. Tell me, if you know, of a people anywhere in history who have contended for more than two hundred years against a superior race, equipped with all the appliances of war and carried on with such a vigor as our war, against the Indian race has been prosecuted. They have contended inch by inch for the land of their fathers, their homes and the burial-grounds of their ancestors.

I am gratified that there is now a feeling of generosity and of respect towards the departing race.

Wanamaker's request was positively received and with the necessary politics complete, Congress acted and the President signed the following act on December 8, 1911:

Be it enacted by the Senate and House of Representatives of the United States of America in Congress assembled. That there may be erected, without expense to the United States Government, by Mr. Rodman Wanamaker, of New York City, and others, on a United States reservation, in the harbor of New York, in the State of New York, and upon a site to be selected by the Secretary of War and the Secretary of the Navy, a suitable memorial to the memory of the North American Indian.

SEC. 2. That for the purpose of carrying out the provisions of this Act a commission, consisting of the chairman of the Committee on the Library of the United States Senate, the chairman of the Committee on the Library of the House of Representatives, the Secretary of War, the Secretary of the Navy, and Mr. Robert C. Ogden, of the city of New York, shall be created, with full authority to select a suitable design, and to contract for the superintend the construction of the said memorial, the design of the memorial to be subjected to the approval of the Commission of Fine Arts.

Rodman Wanamaker was authorized to erect the monument in New York Harbor. The architect of the memorial was to be Thomas Hastings, who had designed the Senate and House office buildings in

Washington D.C., and the Central Research Library of the New York Public Library. Daniel Chester French was to be the sculptor. His works included the Lincoln Memorial in Washington D.C., and the Minute Man, at Concord, Maine, to mention a few. At the base of the monument there was to be a pillared museum. Above was to be a towering bronze Indian. The Indian's hand was to be uplifted with two fingers extended in the universal sign of peace. The statue was to rise 165 feet above the hilltop of Fort Wadsworth on the top of Staten Island, overlooking the Narrows. If completed, this statue would have been bigger than the Statue of Liberty.

It was Washington's birthday, a very symbolic event, with a 21-gun salute, and much singing by the Chiefs who had gathered for this sacred event. Perhaps as a sign of things to come, the day was overcast, and from time to time there was drizzle. Joseph Dixon made the opening speech:

> So far as can be learned, never before in the history of mankind has a monument been erected to a race of people. The ceremonies inaugurating the memorial to the North American Indian are, therefore, pregnant with significance. Over this ground he once roamed, the sea, the sky, the land his patrimony.

> The voices of the past, voices from out of the primeval forest, voices from the far stretches of the Western plains, have been heard, and we are now to realize in granite and bronze an expression of the life of the American people. Posterity will applaud the honor we do ourselves in gathering up the life story of the virile and picturesque race, while yet the rays of the setting sun fall upon their departing footprints.

> The gigantic bronze figure that will surmount the splendid pedestal will face the sea, extending the universal peace sign of the Indian, giving welcome to the nations of the earth as they pass through the greatest gateway to the New World. A lonely, lofty figure, where the sea will forever moan a dirge for a vanished race; where sun and stars, wind and thunder, the gods in his great world-cathedral, may utter the speech of his soul while a child of the woods and plains-but now to fall upon unheeding ears of bronze.

The second speaker that day was the President of the United States. Taft's words are recorded, in part, as follows:

For two centuries the North American Indian has had a right to be treated not as a relic or a prehistoric man but as an existing force, with great and immediate and direct influence upon the settlement and development of this country by the white races and on the course of historical events.

It is appropriate, therefore, that this race which controlled North America for centuries before the white man came here, and that had so much to do with the country since his advent, should have a memorial in this the great sea entrance to the North American continent. Few harbors in the world are more beautiful than that of New York, and here between the upper and lower bays will stand this monument to the red man, recalling his noble qualities, of which he had many, and perpetuating the memory of the succession from the red to the white race in the ownership and control of this Western Hemisphere.

We are indebted to the beneficence of a fellow citizen, Mr. Rodman Wanamaker, through whose generosity this beautiful memorial is to be erected. No monument has a more conspicuous place in the world. At the gate of the New World and facing the old, it tells the story of the march of empire and the progress of Christian civilization to the uttermost limits.

When finished speaking, Taft stepped from the little platform and thrust the spade into the earth. With the soil thus broken, he dug deeper with another implement, an old Indian axe-head found at Tottenville some 30 years previously and believed, according to Dr. George Kunz, "to have been in use by aboriginal hands before Caesar crossed the Rubicon, before ever Agamemnon led the forces outside the walls of Troy."

Then the Great White Father, as they called Mr. Taft, "stepped aside and yielded the ancient Indian tool to Wooden Leg, a muscular warrior chief of the Northern Cheyennes, who bent low and scooped furiously at the soil."

When Wooden Leg finished, White-Man-Runs-Him and the other chiefs came forward, where they each took a rope and together pulled up the stars and stripes. Indian music arranged by Dr. Irving J. Morgan played until the flag was in place. The band then played the "Star Spangled Banner."

Red Hawk of the Sioux spoke next. Then Dr. George Kunz, on behalf of the American Scenic and Historical Preservation Society, produced a bag fresh from the mint. Inside was a new nickel with the head of an American Indian. This new five cent piece was designed to replace the Liberty nickel and honor the American Indian. Taft was given the first nickel from the bag, Wanamaker the second, then all of the chiefs received a coin and finally everyone in the crowd. It was an appropriate time to release this new coin.

Only one humiliating and embarrassing event occurred at Fort Wadsworth. While water had been provided for all of the white guests, none was available in the Indians' headquarters. While little is known about their immediate reaction to this affront, the chiefs apparently forgot the incident quickly. The day after the monument ceremony, the Crow Delegation presented the following declaration to the United States Government:

> We, the undersigned Crow Indians, of Montana, on behalf of our tribe and of the Indians of this Nation as a whole, do, through our presence and the part that we have taken in the dedication of this Memorial to our people, proclaim abroad to all the nations of the world the reassurance of our firm allegiances to this nation and to the stars and stripes, that henceforth and forever, we are in all walks of life and endeavor brothers striving hand in hand."

Respectfully submitted,

F. S. Shively

Robert Yellowtail

Richard Wallace

Plenty Coups (his thumb mark)

Medicine Crow (his thumb mark)

White-Man-Runs-Him (his thumb mark)

Subscribed and sworn to before me this 10th day of February, 1913.

Notary Public D.C.

In addition to the Crow resolution the United Chiefs also presented their declaration:

We, the undersigned representatives of various Indian tribes of the United States, through our presence and the part we have taken in the inauguration of this Memorial to our people, renew our allegiance to the Glorious Flag of the United States, and offer our hearts to our Country's service. We greatly appreciate the honor and privilege extended by our white brothers, who have recognized us by inviting us to participate in the ceremonies on this historical occasion.

The Indian is fast losing his identity in the face of the great waves of Caucasian civilization which are extending to the four winds of this Country, and we want fuller knowledge in order that we may take our places in the civilization which surrounds us.

Though a conquered race, with our right hands extended in brotherly love and our left hands holding the Pipe of Peace, we hereby bury all past ill feelings, and proclaim abroad to all the nations of the world our firm allegiance to this nation and to the Stars and Stripes, and declare that henceforth and forever in all walks of life and every field of endeavor we shall be as brothers, striving hand in hand, and will return to our people and tell them the story of this Memorial and urge upon them their continued allegiance to our common Country.

Before leaving New York the Indian representatives got a tour of the Bronx Zoo. "They spent the most time watching the buffalo and the crocodiles. It was said Plenty Coups spent at least one half hour watching the buffalo. He stared without saying a word even when asked for his thoughts." The delegation then journeyed to tour the Statue of Liberty.

While keeping a busy schedule in New York, White-Man-Runs-Him found time to visit Daniel French, who proceeded to make a plaster cast of the scout. Medicine Crow believes that White-Man-Runs-Him returned to New York several times, even bringing his tepee on one occasion. Chances are he was cast a number of times, and he certainly was used to promote interest in the hoped-for memorial. According to what White-Man-Runs-Him told Winona Plenty Hoops, "It was a terrible experience! First they covered half of my body with white mud clay, then they covered the other half! It was on a long time, and did not feel good. I could not move for some time."

This was potentially a great moment for White-Man-Runs-Him, because it meant he was selected to be the model for the Wanamaker Memorial to the American Indian. Several years earlier ,C. A. Money, a curator for the Smithsonian Institute, had declared that White-Man-Runs-Him "was the best example of the North American Indian, now alive." Having attained the height of 6'4", he stood straight and tall, with all the features and dignity of the perfect plains warrior. On his many expeditions throughout the country, Wanamaker, Joseph Dixon, and their cohorts had taken thousands of pictures. White-Man-Runs-Him stood out as the best person to portray the image hoped for in the Memorial. Whether or not White-Man-Runs-Him was ever paid for his modeling experience is not known.

The Crow and the other tribal representatives' next destination was Philadelphia. They arrived on February 24 at 10:00 a.m. and were welcomed by a brass band and four battalions of cadets who formed an escort as they paraded to the Wanamaker store. They entered Wanamaker's famous Egyptian Hall, where they were treated to a show of the motion pictures taken by Dixon during his western tours. The following day they were welcomed by John Wanamaker, then toured his store, and the city of Philadelphia.

Before leaving Philadelphia, the delegations of Chiefs were given the details of Rodman Wanamaker's upcoming third expedition to the West. This third tour, financed by Wanamaker, would be called a "citizenship" expedition and designed to foster Indian citizenship as well as friendship for the United States. Wanamaker toured by train, which was equipped with photography equipment and a dark room. Thousands of pictures were taken and the stories of Indian leaders recorded. In fact, Dixon wrote the *Vanishing Race* as a result of this tour.

Wanamaker charged himself with carrying the flag hoisted by the chiefs at Fort Wadsworth to each of the 169 Indian nations. Each nation would hoist the flag, then receive flags to fly over their nation. An interesting side-note is that Thomas Edison, a friend of Wanamaker and a supporter of the Indian cause, gave President Wilson the first diamond point portable phonograph ever used. Wilson was asked to make a recording, which he did, to be played at every ceremony. In his recorded speech, Wilson noted: "The Great White Father now calls you his Brother, not his children."

For all of Rodman Wanamaker's apparent interest in Indian affairs, the Wanamaker Memorial was never built. Was it just another in the long history of broken promises to the Indian people or was it something else? No one will probably ever know. White-Man-Runs-Him believed a bronze statue had been cast of him. The Smithsonian does not have it, nor does the Pennsylvania Historic Society, which possesses Wanamaker's records and many of his possessions. Joe Medicine Crow has searched for it for many years. Perhaps a statue or cast was never made. It may be that White-Man-Runs-Him was only convinced that it would be built. He may have confused its construction with the completion of the memorial itself and the bronze statue which would have been created.

Wanamaker left no written record as to why the Memorial was never completed. He may have just transferred his interests to other areas. To a person such as himself who was involved in all aspects of American society, World War I probably seemed more important to him. Thus, in 1914, the Wanamakers chartered a ship, the "Thelma," and asked the people of Philadelphia to supply the cargo for a mission to help relieve the hungry people of Belgium. The "Thelma" sailed on November 11, and one week later was charted with food valued at $150,000.

After the sinking of the "Lusitania," the Wanamakers began a public relations campaign to support the President. On July 27, 1915, John Wanamaker made a speech in which he actually called for the buying of Belgium, for billions if necessary, and then giving the country its freedom. The Wanamakers put Liberty Bonds on sale in their stores and purchased $35 million worth themselves. In 1918, they announced the total gross receipts from the sales of the stores in New York and Philadelphia for five days would be turned over as subscriptions to Liberty Bonds. They advertised for the purchase of Bonds and established overseas bureaus for the forwarding of goods to soldiers at the front. They even initiated a six-and-a-half-hour store day to conserve on energy to aid the war effort.

John Wanamaker died in 1922. Rodman was left to finish the construction of the Wanamaker building in New York, which had been unfinished since 1907, because certain leases had not been completed. Rodman was also busy receiving awards from France, Great Britain, Belgium, Serbia, Paraguay, Uruguay, Venezuela, and the Dominican Republic for his support of them during the war. Being president of a bank, a trustee of an insurance company, executor of estates, and running his business left little time for the memorial. When he died in 1928, so did the idea of a memorial to the American Indian.

Today, Fort Wadsworth is gone. In its place stands the Staten Island terminus of the Verrazano Narrows Bridge. The corner stone of the memorial is missing, but the land designated for the memorial is still reserved for the original purpose. From time to time the idea for a memorial is brought up, but mostly it has been delegated back to the past.

SOURCES

Chapter XI

Appel, Joseph H. *The Business Biography of John Wanamaker Founder and Builder.* New York: The Macmillan Company, 1930.
Contains information on the life and work of John and Rodman Wanamaker.

Keune, Manfred E. "An Immodest Proposal: A Memorial to the North American Indian." A paper presented to the Popular Culture Association, Annual Convention, Baltimore, 1977.
Contains letter to Wilson from Wanamaker, the Congressional act to approve the building of the memorial, the Indian pledge to the United States, an evaluation of Dixon's role in working for Wanamaker, and some information on the memorial.

"Last of Great Indian Chiefs to Gather for Memorial," February 21, 1918.
Uncited news article shows part of the memorial with White-Man-Runs-Him in the foreground. In files of Custer Battlefield National Monument, Crow Agency, Montana.

Medicine Crow, Joe. Personal Interview.
17 June1991.
On his search for the bronze statue.

New York Times, February 23, 1913.
Contains a picture of the monument, speeches, and dedication ceremonies.

New York Tribune, May 29, 1909.
Editorial supporting the building of a National Indian Memorial.

Philadelphia North American, May 14, 1909.
Editorial supports the building of a National Memorial to the American Indian.

Plenty Hoops, Winona. Personal interview.
13 June 1991.
Information on White-Man-Runs-Him being cast.

Reynolds, Charles R. Jr. *American Indian Portraits from the Wanamaker Expedition of 1913.* Brattleboro, Vermont: The Stephen Greene Press, 1971.
Contains some information on Wanamaker's works and expeditions.

Wanamaker, Rodman. *A Tribute to the North American Indian.* New York: The Royeroft Press, 1909.
A brochure authorized by Wanamaker contains speeches given on the memorial, letters of support, and tributes to Bill Cody.

XII. THE CROW DELEGATION OF 1913

The Wanamaker Memorial dedication and the tour of Philadelphia having been completed, the Crow delegation returned to Washington to take care of official business. Prior to leaving the reservation the Crow Council approved the following resolutions:

1. Resolved: that we approved of the request made by the Superintendent, for money from the funds received from sales of ceded lands, to the amount of $40,000 to be used in making the semiannual annuity payment of $25 per capita to all members of the Crow tribe, and request that said funds be furnished as soon as possible.

2. Resolved: that, whereas the Acting Commissioner of Indian Affairs has invited certain prominent men of the Crow tribe, viz Plenty Coups, Medicine Crow, and White-Man-Runs-Him, with Frank Shively as interpreter, to go the city of Washington, to represent the tribe on the occasion of the laying of the cornerstone for a monument to be erected at Washington [New York] to the American Indians, therefore be it:

Resolved: that we hereby express our appreciation of the invitation, as an honor to these men, and we hereby consent to the payment of the necessary expenses for such trip from any Crow funds available.

3. Resolved: that, whereas it has been demonstrated that one threshing outfit cannot handle the grain crop on the Big Horn River, we request that an additional separator and engine be purchased for those districts. Also that an extra engine be purchased for the Pryor district as the one now in use is badly worn and belongs to individual Indians.

4. Resolved: that all completed ditches on the Crow Reservation be completed and a new ditch be constructed on White-Man-Runs-Him Creek and also a new ditch be constructed on Pryor Creek and one be constructed for Reno District.

5. Resolved: that the law firm of Caplar & Merillat of Washington, D.C., be employed as attorneys for the Crow Indians, to have general oversight of all legal affairs of the tribe and to assist the Office of Indian Affairs in any and every way to secure benefits which by right belong to said tribe.

Signatures to the above proceedings were made as follows:
 Ed Wolf Lays Down, *Chairman*
James Hill, Secretary
George W. Hogan,
F. S. Shively,
Sees With His Ears,
Joseph Stewart,
Charles Yarlott,
Frank Shane,
Spotted Rabbit,
Plain Owl,
Medicine Crow,
Bear Don't Walk,
Bull Don't Fall,
 Witnesses to above signatures:
Joseph Martinez,
Frank Hawk.

Superintendent Scott wrote to the Commissioner of Indian Affairs on February 12, approving all resolutions of the Council with the exception of the last two. He questioned the need for a new irrigation ditch because of what he called "prohibitive cost." He said he would review the project and repairs to the existing ditches in the spring. Scott also wrote he knew of no reason to retain the proposed law firm requested by the Council. It seems the Agency always knew what was best for the Crow.

Participation in a Crow delegation to Washington was not new to White-Man-Runs-Him. He had been called to serve before, when he had represented his people in 1910, along with such famous Chiefs as Plenty Coups and Medicine Crow. He had helped plead the case of the Crow who narrowly prevented Congress from opening all Crow tribal land to homesteaders. In part, for his efforts in 1910, White-Man-Runs-Him was appointed Tribal Herald, or Crier, in 1911. His past experience had taught him the procedures used in discussions with the government, and the sometime difficulties of communication and

Famous members of the Crow delegations of 1910 and 1913. (l. to r.) Medicine Crow, White-Man-Runs-Him, Plenty Coups, and Richard Wallace. (Photo courtesy Smithsonian Institute)

Delegation of 1910. (top row) Curley, Plain Owl, White-Man-Runs-Him, Sam Davis (middle row) Packs the Hat, Sees with His Ears, Holds the Enemy, Ar-roches, Spotted Rabbit (front row) Horace Long Bear, Thomas Medicine Horse (Photo courtesy Smithsonian Institute)

real achievement. He was well prepared for his role as a delegate in 1913.

On March 2, the delegation of White-Man-Runs-Him, Plenty Coups, Medicine Crow, Robert Yellowtail, Dick Wallace, and Frank Shively met with Acting Commissioner Abbott at the Indian Office to discuss tribal matters, with Shively acting as interpreter.

Abbott opened the conference by asking what subjects the delegation would like to bring up. Frank Shively then briefly reviewed the questions raised by the tribal council before they left Montana.

Abbott then took over the conference and stated he was concerned about making a $25 payment from the Crow trust funds from the sale of their past ceded land. He worried that Crow funds would soon be gone if payments for supplies and subsistence were given. He argued for using money to purchase a common herd for the Crow rather than purchasing cattle for individuals as last year's delegation had requested Abbott continued by expressing his concern for the elderly, minors, and those he called incompetent to handle their own stock. He told the delegation something was "wrong when people who have so much land as you have, so much irrigated land, and so much grazing land, and are in a condition where you have to ask to withdraw funds to pay for necessities of life." Abbott then looked at each delegate and said he was "sure that none of them needed the money because they were making it on their own."

Abbott was obviously little informed when it came to the economy of the Crow, or he was trying to con them into an accepting mood. He told the delegation he understood "that many people had not been paying their debts, that they had not been living on their allotments, had not been farming, and had not been performing the labor for which they had been paid."

While Abbott indicated he was going to give them the money, he asked the delegation to show the people that per capita payments were coming to an end, and that they must use some of the money to buy seed and farm implements so they could become self-supporting. Abbott ended by saying it was almost time for lunch, butthat he would like to hear from members of the delegation. It seemed to the Crow that the meeting had hardly begun, but they were diplomatic.

Plenty Coups and Medicine Crow spoke on behalf of the payment for the old people. White-Man-Runs-Him spoke as follows:

> You are my commissioner, and I wanted to hear you talk, and I have heard you. That is the reason I came here. Whenever I hear a word which you say it comes into my head and it stays there. I want to thank you for what you have done, and what was said about granting the annuity payments. Whatever you said about the annuity payments is what I say myself. Just as you say, we will be here several days more, and we will have another talk with you, when you have more time. We haven't much time today. You promised to grant me another talk. Now I want to look after our expense money.

White-Man-Runs-Him's concern for funds should have been an indication that the Crow delegation was less than wealthy. The expenses incurred by the delegation had to be paid. During this period of history, it was the responsibility of the tribe to pay for the expenses of the delegates with tribal monies held in trust by Washington. Since the delegation had been away from home for some time, and the Council back in Montana would have to approve the request before any money could be paid, this was a most important issue to the representatives. Abbott listened to the request, but postponed any request for action at that time. White-Man-Runs-Him said no more; he would wait with the others.

Robert Yellowtail then raised a question about canceling certain leases given to white men to enable Indians full use of their range. Abbott stated he believed the leases would take care of themselves and be reduced if the Indians should purchase more cattle.

After some discussion, Abbott told Yellowtail, "The Crow are getting more income from their range today than any other tribe." Yellowtail asked if the Crow added stock, then how long before their income would be quadrupled? Abbott thought it would be five to 10 years. Yellowtail expressed concern over the friction between the Crow and the ranchers over branding each other's cattle and how a number of Crow had landed in jail when they argued or fought the issue. He then asked for a copy of the Congressional Agreement and was presented with the document. The giving of this seemingly complicated agreement to the Crow delegation apparently ended the meeting that day. The Crow would need time to digest the document.

On March 3, the delegation again met with Abbott, this time to request a telegram be sent to Superintendent Scott back at the Crow Reservation requesting five dollars per diem each under the council proceedings of November 25. White-Man-Runs-Him had discussed the issue with the delegation earlier, and they agreed they needed to know their financial status.

Then, together with representatives from 10 other tribes which had gathered at Washington or had been part of the Wanamaker memorial ceremony, the Crow stated their belief that they should take an active part in the inauguration of President Wilson. They argued that their declaration of allegiance to the United States presented the day after the New York monument ceremony qualified them to participate.

Abbott accepted their proposal. The necessary arrangements were taken care of, and on March 5, 1913, the *Washington Post* reported that the crowds cheered the Indian parade entry as much as any other group. Twenty-four Indians rode horses that day. White-Man-Runs-Him, Medicine Crow, and Plenty Coups, were among those listed as riders. The Crow also met with President Wilson, they "looked him in the eye," and they believed he was an honest man.

On March 7, they heard a speech from Secretary of the Interior Lane who told them how responsible they were, how rich they were, how manly they were, how they had taken good care of themselves, and how pleased he was to deal with honest and civilized people who practiced self-restraint.

After several days without business, the Crow returned to meet with Abbott on March 10, to finish their tribal business. Abbott started the meeting with an amendment his office was proposing to Congress:

> Said proceeds (from the sale of ceded lands, etc.) and the interest thereon to be expended for the education, civilization and benefit of said Indians, including the purchase of cattle, to be pro rated to individual members of the tribe in the discretion of the Secretary of the Interior, or the pro rata shares of individual members of the tribe in said funds may be segregated and deposited to their credit in bonded banks and to be expended under such rules and

regulations as may be prescribed by the Secretary of the Interior. The interest provided for these funds while they are in the Treasury is four percent.

According to Abbott:

> If this bill become law, this money may be invested in cattle, or if it is for the better interest of any members of the tribe, they may ask to have it deposited in banks to their credit, and if they are competent to manage their own affairs, the Secretary may turn over that money for them to have in cash, to buy agricultural equipment, build homes, invest in business, or to use in such way as will be for the best interest of the individual. My judgment is that this amendment, as it now stands, is one of the very best pieces of legislation that has ever been recommended for any tribe of Indians. I have given it my very best thought, and I have tried to get this amendment so that it will give us plenty of freedom to handle this fund for the very best interest of the Crow people. I think I have covered every point now in connection with your leases and this bill, which it is important to cover, and I am ready now to turn over the letter and the copies of all of our discussions to you.

Abbott then tried to discourage the Crow from staying in Washington until April when Congress was to meet in special session. He told the Crow the amendment might not be discussed until next December and the financial cost to the tribe would be too great. He suggested rather that they could meet to talk with Senators and Representatives to gain support for the amendment.

The delegation then discussed the various interpretations of the pending bill. The Crow wanted their Montana agent to have quicker access to money so that the delays of the Washington bureaucracy could be prevented. Abbott said once he received requests, they were out of his office within three days. Yellowtail disputed the speed of Abbott's office, saying he talked to a number of people who seemed to know nothing or were confused about things that were to pass through them. Abbott appeared to answer questions about the slowness of government by saying the Crow didn't understand how the system works.

Discussion now moved to a concern by the Crow that annuity inheritances took too long to get to the deceased relatives. They didn't like the hearings and all the paper work back and forth from Montana to Washington.

As the discussion ensued, Yellowtail asked what it cost to run the Crow Reservation. Abbott asked for the report and it was read as follows by a Mr. Dimick:

(These figures are from "Indian Moneys, Proceeds of Labor")

Salaries and wages	$20,026.96
Transportation of persons	995.60
Transportation of supplies	103.01
Subsistence and support of persons	1,228.05
Subsistence and care of animals	5.50
Communication service (telephone and telegraphing),	.70
Printing, engraving, binding, etc.	2.75
Advertising and publication of notices	93.19
Materials not specifically adapted for use as supplies, equipment, or structures	418.92
Stationery, drafting, scientific and educational supplies	1,040.86
Fuel	1,3,246.69
Mechanic's supplies	124.50
Cleaning and toilet supplies	5.01
Wearing apparel, sewing supplies, etc.	23.70
Forage	4,594.12
Provisions	479.14
Equipment and material for equipment	8,869.74
Structures and material for structures	13,460.66
Miscellaneous	440.40
Total	$55,159.50

The Crow listened to the figures with apparently no comments being made. The meeting ended when Abbott said he would consider the Crow request to allot money to children born after 1905.

The discussion with Abbott continued on March 15. The Crow delegation was interested in buying cattle as soon as possible. In fact, they wanted to use some of their money to buy outright the Frank Heinrich lease. Yellowtail spoke in favor of each person owning his own cattle to make people more responsible for them. Abbott asked if the law would allow this. "Would you rather have tribal cattle or none at all?" The Crow seemed to want the tribal cattle in that event.

Plenty Coups was concerned that the cattle be purchased as soon as possible. He also wanted to purchase local cattle because it was their home, and they wouldn't stray. The Crow were concerned that the current laws would force them to buy southern cattle, and they wanted to be free to do as they choose with their money. White-Man-Runs-Him added,

> Plenty Coups' argument should not be changed. That is the argument that is strongly in our favor, and he really outlined that which all the rest of us had to say. I believe that with the rest, that we should push this bill through Congress as fast as we can, and in the meantime proceed to use the funds available to purchase cattle immediately; to take immediate steps to purchase the cattle on the reservation. With respect to the funds that are in the Treasury, aside from those with which the bill has to do, should we buy cattle with those, do I understand you that we can divide them pro rata?

Abbott replied, "Which? The cattle bought with the income from the grazing fund, for instance?" Robert Yellowtail answered, "Yes sir." and Abbott agreed.

White-Man-Runs-Him spoke again saying,

> I wish with the rest to push that as fast as we can through Congress, and proceed with this other, and when it passes, we then buy more cattle and use more range. I want to substantiate a little more, if I can, the argument of Plenty Coups saying that the cattle which are natives of the reservation are well-bred stock and know the water holes, which is a great factor in the breeding proposition and the best ranges and are acclimated, so that we need not fear that they will die the first year or not have the proper increase the first year of calves.

The discussion then returned to allotment of money to the children, and White-Man-Runs-Him spoke for the Crow:

> I wish to remind you that the children who were born since Mr. Rankin completed his allotment work are now grown, as you might say. There have been a great many, and the first ones are quite large. That has been 13 years ago. It seems that they ought to be entitled to an allotment now, so that if improvements and fencing is desired, we can go right ahead with it. There are some good places left which might be selected and allotted, and I thought it would be advisable if we could get some of a rule by which we could start the allotment work immediately again. They are Crows like the rest of us; they are not coyotes or animals chasing around without any land; and they are entitled to land just like the rest of us. You are Commissioner and can bring about the allotment so that they can have land of their own. When we have any amount of stock it is always to our interests, and we make it our business to provide for them the best we can. There are 1700 of us and you are our chief, our destinies are with you. You are at the head, and it is your duty to take the initiative and straighten out these things for us.

Abbott replied, "Plenty Coups has already raised that question, and I have promised to look that up and answer him."

White-Man-Runs-Him added, "This friction has been happening ever since Mr. Rankin completed his allotment work. The corners which he showed us — he showed us our corners and we stuck sticks down. After he went away and we were issued our plats, in many cases they were not exactly as he showed us. We have had trouble among ourselves in regard to our corners. If there is any way to straighten out that when the new allotment agent comes, that would help us."

Richard Wallace then expressed another Crow concern: "Some of the agricultural lands which are supposed to be in the ditch, where our homes are, and the grazing lands are allotted sometimes as much as 10 miles away from them, and it breaks up the allotment and it is very inconvenient. It makes us go away off to our grazing land. Where it is practicable, could the Office fix it so that we could change to get unoccupied lands which adjoin our own agricultural lands?"

Abbott agreed allotments could be exchanged, "but there would have to be a clear reason to justify it."

As the March 15 conference concluded, White-Man-Runs-Him commented, "I realize that we had a better meeting this time than any we have had. Mr. Abbott, I want you to jump in ahead and help us all that you can."

Medicine Crow agreed, "I helped the soldiers when they were in trouble. Mr. Abbott, jump in and help me." White-Man-Runs-Him made the final comment. "We made a collection to buy a tract of land, 40 acres or 20 acres, for a fair grounds. I wish to always reserve that if there is any way to do that. We paid our money out for that. I want you to know that so in case you should ever have anything about that you would know of it."

On March 17, Scott wired the Crow delegation that the Indian Council would only authorize $3 per diem and not the $5 as requested for their stay in Washington. After the delegation was informed, they turned to the agenda that was set for them.

The agenda for March 17 was recorded as follows:

Conference between F. H. Abbott, Acting Commissioner of Indian Affairs, and a delegation of Crow Indians consisting of:
Plenty Coups
White-Man-Runs-Him
Medicine Crow
Richard Wallace
Robert Yellowtail
Frank Shively (Interpreting).
Regarding:
Approval of expenditure of $15,000 for stallions,
Protest against expenditure of $40,000 for sheep,
Purchase of cattle,
Reimbursable fund,
Hospital,
Trust Fund,
Detail of Mr. Goodall,
Buying of Frank Heinrich's cattle,
Allotment of children,
Per diem payment to delegation,
Pension for White-Man-Runs-Him, as Miles' Scout,

The delegation quickly approved the use of $15,000 to purchase horses, but they objected strongly to the purchase of sheep. They wanted the law changed so the $40,000 could be used for other purposes.

Abbott then informed the Crow he could give them $400,000 for the purchase of cattle. When the amendment passed Congress, Abbott told them they would have another $240,000 which was tied up for the purchase of southern cattle, and the $40,000 which had been set up for sheep. He also told them they would be able to divide the cattle up among individuals.

Abbott also came up with $50,000 for loans to those who wanted to improve their allotments. The Superintendent was to be in charge of the loans. One man could borrow only up to $600. Abbott also said that there would be $10,000 for the erection of a hospital; $50,000 would be invested with the interest being used to maintain the hospital, and $100,000 was also to be invested and the interest used in any way the Crow wanted.

Abbott then said he would send a Mr. Goodall, a livestock inspector, to the Crow Reservation to consult with them. He also suggested the Crow form a business council.

While the Crow were generally happy with the results of the meetings, much discussion took place over the breed of horses to purchase, and the fact that there would not be enough money to purchase the entire Heinrich herd.

As the conference came to a close, White-Man-Runs-Him finished the session by saying, "The tribal affairs have been talked over now, and I want to talk to you about a personal matter. I and two or three others who were Scouts for General Miles ought to receive pensions, the same as soldiers of the United States Army. I want you to look after that."

Abbott consented to "make a note of that and look that matter up and write him a letter about that."

On March 20, Abbott and the Crow met again but only to say friendly good-byes. Abbott wrote a letter to the Crow, who returned to Montana on March 24, in which he denied any further allotments to children, explaining that allotments could be exchanged through the Superintendent who would do the paperwork. He also explained that the Superintendent should solve boundary problems, and that he could find no record which indicated the Crow had purchased 40 acres near Pryor, known as Plenty Coups Race Track, for a fair grounds.

On March 31, White-Man-Runs-Him received the following letter from Abbott:

Education-Law & Order
35517-1913
F H D
Claim for pension.

Mr. White-Man-Runs-Him,
Through Supt. Crow School.

Sir:

In connection with the conference held in this Office wherein you refer to the service of yourself and others as scouts for General Miles, and suggest that you should receive pensions the same as the soldiers of the U. S. Army, a full and complete statement should be furnished showing just what service was rendered, for what period, whether you were wounded or contracted disease in the service, and line of duty, and such other information as will enable the Office to find out whether you have a pensionable status and whether the facts are such as to make it advisable to endeavor to procure a special act in your behalf. Please furnish all information possible on the subject.

Respectfully,

3-AB-25
Acting Commissioner

The business of the 1913 Crow delegation was finally concluded on July 14, by letter, with approval given to Superintendent Scott to purchase a threshing separator for $2,150. The Crow request first was made on February 7. While the delegation did not achieve everything they sought, they did make progress. Even though the official notes do not indicate it, the Crow were tough negotiators. Each time a delegation went to Washington, it learned a great deal about the politics of the white man and how to deal with it. Washington's respect for Crow ideas, goals, and needs would increase as the years went by.

White-Man-Runs-Him returned as a delegate to Washington in 1914, but was not counted among those delegates elected from the Crow Tribal Districts who attended the famous delegations of 1917 headed by Chief Plenty Coups. White-Man-Runs-Him had been with the delegation of 1910 which began the battle to overturn Lone Wolf vs Hitchcock, the Supreme Court 1903 decisions that authorized Congress to open for white settlement, the tribal lands of any Indian tribe when deemed necessary for the public good, regardless of any treaty stipulations to the contrary.

With almost all representatives of Montana in the early Twentieth Century in agreement, Senator Thomas Walsh of Montana led the charge to open the Crow reservation. Walsh favored opening the reservation to small homestead settlement. White-Man-Runs-Him confronted Senator Walsh during a number of hearings on both the federal and state levels. Joe Medicine Crow remembers on one such occasion, Walsh kept asking White-Man-Runs-Him a number of questions all relating to the size of the reservation and the amount of land the Crow had or needed for their relatively small population. White-Man-Runs-Him finally said, "You want me to say that the Crow own too much land, you want me to say yes, we have too much land, but I will not say it. We have lost too much land already. As time passes on, we may need yet more."

The 1917 Crow delegation was to meet with the Senate Indian Affairs Committee for the final hearing before the bill went to the Senate. If the bill were passed, it would mean an end to the Crow way of life. It was to be a great moment for the Crow people. On April 5, the night before the hearing, Plenty Coups called for the delegates to meet in their hotel to make an appeal to the traditional war medicines for help in defeating the proposed bill.

The old chiefs went to the city zoo and gathered buffalo chips for their burnt offerings. The rest of the ingredients had been brought with them to Washington. They sat in a semicircle in their room, with their war medicines and fighting regalia spread out before them. Plenty Coups told the group, "This is not a sham of medicine; aid-asking rituals were always engaged in just before charging into the enemy. Right now we are preparing to fight a different kind of fight."

The ceremony would help them in their struggle as an enemy was making raids on them. "We must fight to protect our women and children."

The old chiefs then recounted the Crow migration and war history with a variety of tribes. They declared their war exploits and prepared to fight an enemy superior in numbers on his home turf. While this was not new to the Crow, this time they would have to fight with words, many of which they did not understand.

The ceremony must have been impressive. The buffalo chips were burned along with sweet grass and nez perce roots. Wood coals were used to burn the incense. Smoke filled the room. Each chief prayed after stirring the medicine herbs, then sang his war song. The ceremony was finished when Plenty Coups directed Robert Yellowtail who was the mouthpiece of the Crow. He told Yellowtail, "You will reply to Senator Walsh tomorrow and I don't want any of the rest of you to interrupt as we are staking our all on what he will say, and do tomorrow...do your best tomorrow...our Crow tribe's salvation is in your hands now."

Yellowtail was up to the task. In a brilliant speech, he turned the Senate hearing into one of silent reflection. When Yellowtail had finished, Senator LaFollette from Wisconsin and others rose to support the Crow. The Chairman asked Walsh if he wished to poll the Senate Committee. He stated, "Mr. Chairman, it is plainly useless to do that. I am convinced that this Committee is opposed to my bill and I therefore withdraw my bill and I humbly acknowledge defeat at the hands of Robert Yellowtail who has pleaded their defense." Walsh never again supported the opening of the Crow land. The National Hotel had witnessed the last time the Crow would invoke their traditional war medicines to achieve victory. White-Man-Runs-Him would have enjoyed the moment. Upon the delegation's return, he participated in the victory dances held throughout the reservation.

While it took until 1920 for Congress to finally approve the work started by White-Man-Runs-Him, Medicine Crow, and Plenty Coups in 1910, the efforts and struggles of the Crow did finally pay off. The bill that became law in 1920 provided that the reservation would be divided among all members of the tribe; it would eliminate any wholesale opening of Crow land; it would eliminate the Crow from having to depend on the Indian officers when it came to administering their property; and it stipulated that tribal money would go to the individual landowners.

However, White-Man-Runs-Him did indirectly participate in the famous delegation of 1917. After the delegates had been elected, two Crow men, according to a letter received by the Indian Office in Washington, from Superintendent Estep at the Crow Agency, "left for Washington in the interest of the opening bill. One man was under bond for appearance before Federal Grand Jury on charge of introducing liquor, giving some to school boys and had recently paid a fine in state court for being drunk in Hardin. The other man was not noted for any honorable work and was flashing big bills." In several other letters of correspondence, the implication was that these men had been paid off by business interests in Billings to encourage the opening of the reservation to homesteaders. There were also implications the two men had gained signatures to a petition by telling people they were signing for increased annuity rates when really they had signed statements requesting the opening.

White-Man-Runs-Him's name appears second on a petition to Washington dated January 8, 1917, stating that the two men were not legal delegates and that they should not be paid, accepted as delegates, or returned to the reservation by the government. While the two men under question were exposed through such correspondence, they would be accepted later as delegates, the reasons for their acceptance being unclear. White-Man-Runs-Him abided by the rules, and he wished for the same in others.

SOURCES

CHAPTER XII

Superintendent's Annual Narrative and Statistical Reports, Records Group 75, National Archives.
Contains correspondence and minutes of the proceedings of delegations.

Yellowtail, Robert Summers Sr. *Robert Summers Yellowtail Sr.* Albuquerque: Cold Type Service of New Mexico, 1973.
Story of the war ceremonies of the 1917 delegation.

XIII. A SENSE OF HISTORY

From the time of the Battle at the Little Big Horn until his death, White-Man-Runs-Him developed a keen sense and interest in history, especially concerning the Crow Nation and the events leading up to and surrounding the battle at Little Big Horn. As he sought answers to unanswered questions and discussed his views and knowledge as a scout, his notoriety spread. In pursuit of a greater understanding of the fight at the Little Big Horn, he often traveled to Lame Deer, the nearby Cheyenne Reservation, to council with Cheyenne and Sioux warriors who had fought against Custer. Wherever he was called to participate in a ceremony or represent his people, he took the opportunity to discuss aspects of the Indian-White Wars. He raised questions and shared information, never turning down the opportunity to communicate his knowledge of the conflict. He never received any compensation from the numerous authors or curiosity seekers who placed demands on his time. Joe Medicine Crow believes that he was given "some smokes or a plug of tobacco" by some people who visited him, but these items were not of much use since White-Man-Runs-Him did not smoke for pleasure, chew tobacco, or drink.

White-Man-Runs-Him walked the Custer Battlefield and retraced his steps as a scout so many times it is impossible to determine his investment in time. While not all of the authors listened to him as well as they might have, he knew well, and advised General E. S. Godfrey, General Hugh Scott, Herbert Coffeen, Col. Tim Mc Coy, E. A. Brinstool, Col. Henry Harrington, Col. W. A. Graham, Frank Linderman, Edward S. Curtis, Fred Dustin, Coe Hayne, C. A. Woodruff, Joseph Dixon, and Thomas Marquis to name a few.

Few authors during his life wrote about Custer without consulting White-Man-Runs-Him. Letters of correspondence indicate people of reputation looked forward with great anticipation and excitement to visiting with him when they headed for Montana. A letter written by Robert Bruce to General Godfrey on August 15, 1928, states he had

WHITE-MAN-RUNS-HIM
The last of the four famous Crow Scouts attached to the command of
Major-General George A. Custer at the Battle of the Little Big Horn

Pictures for postcards were often taken of White-Man-Runs-Him. It is uncertain as to whether he was ever paid for such photos. (Photo from the Medicine Crow files.)

"just spent some time with Mrs. Custer" and that he had "just talked to Col. Bates who was headed west where he expected to see White-Man-Runs-Him."

In 1928, a year before his death, White-Man-Runs-Him quoted from memory, to author Coe Hayne, the names of all of the Crow Scouts who had originally enlisted with Gibbon, and their roles through the battle at the Little Big Horn. In 1919, he led General Hugh Scott and Lt. Varnum to the original Crow's Nest. The exact location of the Crow's Nest, where he sighted the Sioux camp on the Little Big Horn, had been lost for some 55 years. Historians prior to 1919, had used the wrong peak in developing their theories on the battle. White-Man-Runs-Him pointed out "he could see both the Sioux Camp and the Custer camp of the day before" near Busby, Montana. Interestingly enough, the site of the Crow's Nest was then lost again until Henry Weibert and William Boyles rediscovered it in 1972.

Joe Medicine Crow was about 12 years old when his stepfather, John White-Man-Runs-Him (son of White-Man-Runs-Him), arranged an interview for Thomas Marquis with his father. While there is little doubt White-Man-Runs-Him understood English, he never spoke it. He was an expert at sign language and always requested an interpreter, in this case, members of his family.

During the course of the interview, Marquis and White-Man-Runs-Him discussed the battle at the Little Big Horn including the possibility that a number of Custer's soldiers might have committed suicide. Marquis, who worked as a doctor among the Sioux and Cheyenne, interviewed many of the warriors who fought against Custer, and many believed a mystic power had caused the soldiers' death. They told Marquis that an invisible wall had been thrown up around the troopers reflecting the bullets back to the "aggressors." Many Indians had talked about the soldiers "gone crazy," who had aimed their guns in the wrong direction. Had the undisciplined and panicky soldiers, fearing capture and torture, followed the old frontier proverb: "When fighting Indians, keep the last bullet for yourself"? White-Man-Runs-Him knew these stories well. He heard them many times, but he remained silent as to his view on this matter.

For years, White-Man-Runs-Him was asked for his viewpoint on the whereabouts of Curley during the Custer fight. It was Curley who delivered the message to the supply boat, "Far West," that Custer had been defeated. Curley became a much publicized scout in the aftermath of the battle. It was often reported that he was the only survivor, observing the battle, only to escape by using a Sioux blanket. Many of the stories about him and his role were fabricated, made up by white men who would not listen to or had misinterpreted what Curley said. White-Man-Runs-Him, Goes Ahead, and Hairy Moccasin always stood by their stories of how Curley had left with the Arikara scouts sometime before the sighting of the Lone Tepee. White-Man-Runs-Him said, "Curley left us up on Reno Creek. He left with the Arikara and the horses. They went to the Rosebud junction up by Lame Deer. They were there by evening where the Rosebud flows into the Yellowstone. The Arikara told me that Curley was with them."

Curley never maintained he was in the battle, but his last story given to Russell White Bear stated: "Bouyer called me to him – he said – Curley you better leave us here – You ride back over the trail a ways and then go to one of the high points [pointing eastward over to the high ridge east of the Custer Hill] – watch awhile and tell him we are killed." Curley then claimed to have climbed a hill and observed the battle from about a mile and a half away with his glasses. Then he rode away.

LeForge reported that he talked to Curley near Gibbon's base camp on the Yellowstone the day after the battle on the 26th. Curley asked where Gibbon was, then rode off upstream without telling LeForge about the battle. Later Curley said he was "so dull and sleepy that he thought by that time everyone knew the outcome." Curley reported to the "Far West" in the afternoon. The controversy on where Curley was still goes on. One thing seems certain – he was not with White-Man-Runs-Him, Goes Ahead, and Hairy Moccasin. Tension existed for years between Curley and the other scouts concerning credibility regarding what they knew of the battle.

White-Man-Runs-Him enjoyed telling stories involving interesting sidelights to the Custer fight. Lee Old Mouse of Busby, Montana, told Joe Medicine Crow one such story concerning the horse of Bloody Knife, a scout who was killed when he was shot in the head during the battle of the Little Big Horn. Bloody Knife's horse had been shot many times with arrows during the engagement. Frightened, the horse left the field of conflict and traveled some 1,000 miles back to Bloody Knife's Arikara camp, in North Dakota. When the horse arrived at the camp, arrows still protruded from its back. The villagers recognized the horse immediately as that of Bloody Knife. The Arikara cleaned the wounds of the horse and nursed it back to health. From that time on, no one ever again rode this very special animal. The horse was given its own war song and always had a special place in Arikara celebrations and parades.

The whiskey question discussed earlier also never left White-Man-Runs-Him. It bothered him because it appeared that the authors of the time either ignored the Crow viewpoint or refused to take seriously the fact that Custer's troops had not only consumed alcohol several times prior to the battle, but also in some cases filled their canteens with it. It further upset him when whiskey was brought by boat or by pack horses to Miles and others he campaigned with. Why would the white authors go to great lengths to try and prove Custer's forces did not have access to whiskey, while the journals of other military campaigns and those who wrote about the campaigns freely mentioned the whiskey breaks? In the words of White-Man-Runs Him, "It made no sense."

Another question White-Man-Runs-Him constantly dealt with concerned why the Crow scouts were released by Custer. The evidence supports, and the Crow scouts repeated, that from the time they first met Custer, he told them that their job was to find the Sioux, and he [Custer] would fight them. While on the trail, Custer told the scouts on a number of occasions their job was done once the Indians were discovered. In fact, a traditional army approach when employing Indian scouts was to use them to chase off the enemy's horses or to release the scouts. Many commanders believed Indians were difficult to command because they fought as individuals, thus making military strategy difficult for them to execute.

The Crow elders discussed the Custer release of the scouts for a number of years and always came to the same conclusion. It was their view Custer really liked these scouts; they were very young and had been totally honest with him. In fact, they had been correct in reading the signs and informing Custer of the overwhelming odds which awaited him. The scouts were prepared to die. They had dressed for battle and sung their songs. They were somewhat confused and frustrated during the final moments. Two of the scouts who should have been with Custer, White Swan and Hairy Moccasin, left with Reno because they had misunderstood or did not hear the orders from the translator in the confusion before battle. To the Crow elders, Custer released the young Crow scouts because at the final moment, Custer knew what the end result would be, and he wished to save these "innocent ones."

Historians constantly bombarded White-Man-Runs-Him with questions of "Who killed Custer? Where was he killed? Was he brave until the end? Was he the last man standing?" To White-Man-Runs-Him, the white concept of battle and the questions were hard to understand at first. As time passed, he came to realize about such interests and sought to seek the answers, even though he himself could not testify to such events.

White-Man-Runs-Him talked to the Sioux and the Cheyenne and listened to their stories. He discovered there were many stories, and that each person saw the battle from his own perspective, and location. Some Indians told White-Man-Runs-Him they knew who Custer was and they knew he was coming, for they had tracked him for many miles. Others said they did not know it was Custer they were fighting, and some said that they were surprised to see soldiers come over the hill. Still others said they knew an army was coming, but didn't believe they would attack before first seeking a truce and negotiating. Many thought that the large size of their camp was their security and only a fool would dare attack them.

White-Man-Runs-Him wondered about the communications within the Sioux and Cheyenne camp. He himself had talked with their scouts on the trail. They knew the soldiers were coming, and they certainly knew of the soldiers whereabouts for some time before the battle. A young boy had been killed; smoke from the soldiers' camps must have been seen; and the Arikara had chased several warriors who must have warned the village, but again there were many opinions.

White-Man-Runs-Him was certain he saw Custer go into the ford. After his observation White-Man-Runs-Him left the field. Custer was brave to the end. He must have been brave to charge the force that lay before him. White Tail Bull, who fought against Custer, said that Custer charged the river, then suddenly stopped because he believed the leader had been shot and had fallen from his horse into the stream. The soldiers retrieved the leader, then charged again. John B. Cummings, a Crow elder, was interviewed by Joe Medicine Crow in 1965, and told him the following story was given to him by David Holley, an Assiniboine, from Fort Belknap Reservation:

> When General Custer and his men were entering the Little Big Horn River to cross it, the Indians, both Cheyenne and Sioux, counterattacked. Some soldiers fell into the swollen river; others turned and headed for the ridge. A Sioux warrior named Spotted Antelope was one of the first to cross the river and started pursuing the soldiers up the hill. Spotted Antelope caught up with General Custer, who now found himself in the rear of his men, and bashed him over the head with a tomahawk. As the General tumbled off his horse, another Sioux named Black Bear came up and took Custer's horse. And as Custer hit the ground, other warriors shot at him. At this point, a Sioux Indian, a hunting and drinking partner of Custer's, came and took charge of the body. He rolled his friend in his robe and forbade anybody molesting his friend's body. About this time it was reported that the last group on the hill were all killed and the battle was over. This man then put the body of General Custer on a horse and took it up the hill and left it with the last of the fallen soldiers.

A Sioux chief named White Bull told Stanley Vestel, in 1932, how he had killed Custer in hand to hand combat. According to White Bull, he wrestled with Custer at a time when there were only 10 or so men remaining alive on the hill. He said he finally killed him by hitting Custer with Custer's own pistol that he wrenched away from him in the fight.

Several other Indians claimed to have killed Custer. Some did so perhaps because money had been offered to the person who would come forward and tell who had killed Custer. Many Indians were afraid to tell the white man what they knew of the battle for fear of repercussions. One Indian admitted to killing Custer while members of his tribe listened to his story. When he was alone with his people later on, they challenged him as to why he said he did something he did not do. He answered by explaining it was what the white man wanted to hear, and it was not wrong to lie to a white man. Rain in the Face, a famous Sioux Chief, believed Custer committed suicide. Kate Bighead, who was at the battle, told the story of Monahseetah [alleged former lover of Custer], and another Cheyenne woman who saw Custer's body on the field, prevented its mutilation, then washed the body and placed it in its final resting place. Before they left the field, they pierced Custer's ears with an awl so his hearing would improve in the great beyond. He had not listened before when he was warned by the Cheyenne not to break his word. Custer was found by the soldiers in a position they described as a "man who had fallen asleep," with a peaceful appearance, his arms spread out across the bodies of two other men. Was he placed in this position?

Another story told by Clara Bull Tail, a Crow, to Willard Fraser, describes how when Custer attacked Black Kettle's camp on the Washita, he used his sword to cut off the breast of a woman nursing her baby. Both mother and baby died shortly after. According to Clara Bull Tail, the grandmother of the child was at the battle. A Cheyenne warrior found Custer still alive as the battle neared its end. The warrior recognized Custer and called to the Cheyenne woman, who then brought Beaver Not-Afraid, to see the man who killed her daughter and grandchild. Beaver Not-Afraid, seeing Custer was quickly dying, called for someone to get the "fat one," a Cheyenne woman who was so overweight that she needed to be pulled on a travois. The "fat one" was brought to where Custer lay, as quickly as possible. "Breathless, she raised her skirt, and plunked her bare backside down squarely on Custer's face, where she proceeded to sit and smother him into eternity."

Such were the stories that White-Man-Runs-Him had heard. He could relate them all, but could not testify to any with absolute certainty. That Custer was killed early in the fight seemed to make sense, for he always led the way.

Even though White-Man-Runs-Him continued to help those interested in Custer, he found time to raise his family. He began to increase his farming endeavors, adding some cattle to compliment his horse business. He increased production on his land by planting oats and hay. He was able to save some money and established a savings account in the Wyola Bank. He added to his income through participation in local and regional parades. He was much in demand,

Max Big Man (left) and White-Man-Runs-Him. They often discussed the history and culture of the Plains. (Photo courtesy National Battlefield Archives, Crow Agency, Montana.)

and it was noted by one newspaper that reported his death: "He will be much missed at parades and fairs."

Winona Plenty Hoops said she remembered with fond memories the family packing up and leaving home for as much as two weeks to attend a parade in Sheridan. White-Man-Runs-Him traveled to fairs and parades in his wagon pulled by a team. It took the team several days to get to Sheridan, and the family enjoyed camping along the way. White-Man-Runs-Him was especially proud of his team, consisting of a bay and a strawberry roan. The bay was very gentle around people, especially children. It was a special horse. When it came time for the parade, the horse seemed to sense a show as it was brushed and groomed. Feathers were tied to its tail and it was handsomely decorated. When White-Man-Runs-Him mounted the horse and the music started, the bay came to life. The horse raised its legs with excitement and moved down the parade route, prancing proudly.

White-Man-Runs-Him was present in 1902 for the 26th reenactment of the Custer Battle, and he was there in 1916 and again in 1926 for the 50th anniversary. Some 6,000 people attended the ceremony, with 2,100 coming by rail from Billings, Miles City, and Sheridan in special trains. In 1902, he advised and participated in the reenactment of the battle itself. In 1916, no reenactment of the battle took place, but there was much fanfare. Everyone made a speech; Mrs. Custer was there and presented a picture of her husband to the National Cemetery. White-Man-Runs-Him also made a brief speech through his interpreter, Russell White Bear. He stood on the speaker's stand which was placed on an automobile and said, "Forty years ago enemies met here. Today all meet as friends. We pay honor to the great yellow-haired chieftain. It is good."

In 1923, White-Man-Runs-Him was invited to attend the Shrine Imperial [national convention], held in Washington D.C. There doesn't seem to be a record of which temple he represented; however, it is known that he participated in the Shrine parade and other celebrations of the Shrine. It seems likely that he represented Al Bedoo Temple, from Billings, Montana. Richard Beulke, Al Bedoo Temple recorder, notes that the Temple minutes of 1923, state: "Distribution of some kind of favors to others attending the session were granted." It may have been a member or members of the Temple helped pay the way for White-Man-Runs-Him, his adopted daughter Clara, her husband, Winona, and her brother. Winona recalls meeting President Harding, and being greatly impressed by the city and the events of the convention. Harding even took time to show the family his typewriter and how it worked. Pretty Medicine Pipe, White-Man-Runs-Him's wife, had been to Washington before and did not wish to attend the convention in 1923.

White-Man-Runs-Him continued to be in demand as an honored person, and whenever possible, tried to meet the needs of the occasion. He was much photographed, with his picture appearing in National Geographic several times in 1926. He unveiled the monument at Garry Owen and participated in a multitude of dedications throughout Montana and Wyoming. Even when his health began to fail him in old age, White-Man-Runs-Him seemed to gain energy and come alive when he was sought out. His desire to help out whenever possible won for him the accolades of all who knew him.

Ceremonies at the National Battlefield, Crow Agency, Montana. Pretty Medicine Pipe is on the left beside White-Man-Runs-Him. (Photo courtesy of the National Battlefield Archives, Crow Agency, Montana.)

White-Man-Runs-Him offers a prayer at the National Battlefield, 1926. (Photo courtesy of the National Battlefield Archives, Crow Agency, Montana.)

SOURCES

Chapter XIII

Dippie, Brian W., "The Thrillin'est Fight Ever." *Annals of Wyoming,* Vol. 54, No. 2, 1982.
On re-enactment of Battle at the Little Big Horn.

Fraser, Willard E. "A Squaw Did Custer In?" *Billings Gazette,* August, 22, 1969.

Hanner, Kenneth. *Men With Custer.* Old Army Press, 1972.
Contains biographies of the Seventh Cavalry and all of the scouts.

Ketcham, Barbara. "New finds shed light on Custer's Last Stand." *Star-Tribune,* Casper, Wyoming, March 30, 1975.
Contains information on the discovery of the Crow's Nest.

LeForge, Thomas. *Memoirs of a White Crow Indian.* Lincoln and London: University of Nebraska, 1974.
Contains information about seeing Curley after the Little Big Horn.

Letter received from Richard A. Beulke, Al Bedoo Temple, Ancient order Nobles of Mystic Shrine, Billings, Montana, October 14, 1991.
Information might mean Shriners sent White-Man-Runs-Him to the National Convention in Washington.

Letter written by Robert Bruce, author, to General Godfrey, August 15, 1928. In files of National Battlefield, Crow Agency, Montana.

Marquis. Thomas B. *Keep The Last Bullet For Yourself.* Algonac, Michigan: Reference Publications, Inc., 1976.
Marquis theories of suicide.

Medicine Crow, Joe. Personal interview.
15 June 1991.
Marquis interview and discussion with White-Man-Runs-Him.

Medicine Crow, Joe. "Statement of John B. Cummings." Mimeographed: June 25, 1983.
Contains David Halley's account of Custer's death as relayed to Cummings.

New York Herald, June 6, 1909.
Contains pictures of White-Man-Runs-Him and the other scouts and focuses on the fight at Little Big Horn.

Plenty Hoops, Winona. Personal interview.
13 June 1991.
Memories and stories about White-Man-Runs-Him.

Richards, Raymond. "Picturesque Celebration of Red Men's Last Trimuph in the West is Given Where Custer Offered Full Measure." *Billings Journal,* June 26, 1916.
Contains White-Man-Runs-Him speech to those gathered for the 40th anniversary.

Stewart, Edgar I. *Custer's Luck.* Norman: University of Oklahoma Press, 1957.
The Curley story.

XIV. SEEKING A PENSION

As a member of the Crow Delegation to Washington in 1913, White-Man-Runs-Him first requested that he and scouts like him be given a pension. At that time he did not qualify. Then in 1917, Congress passed the appropriate legislation. Under Congressional Acts of July 27, 1892, June 27, 1902, and May 30, 1908, pensions were provided for veterans of a number of United States conflicts. Then on March 17, 1917, the above acts were extended to include pensions "To survivors of certain wars and disturbances with and campaigns against Indians from 1817 to 1891, inclusive, and to their widows."

This act included the campaign against the Northern Cheyennes and the Sioux in 1876 and 1877. Widows of such veterans were included if they had married the veteran 30 days or more prior to March 4, 1917. The rate of pension was set by the government at $20 per month. For White-Man-Runs-Him this meant that he would now have the opportunity to gain a pension, which would make his life somewhat easier.

White-Man-Runs-Him filled out his Declaration for Pension, Indian Wars form, on November 21, 1921. He was, according to the form, 67 years of age. The declaration was a basic statement, including identification of his former unit, his job with Custer and Miles, and his personal description at the time of his employment by the army. He listed his current occupation as a hunter and farmer. His declaration was made before L.C. Rennich, Notary Public, residing at the Crow Agency. White-Man-Runs-Him signed the declaration with his thumbprint.

Approximately three months later, White-Man-Runs-Him received and filled out a second form. The form was a fee contract provided by the Commissioner of Pensions without cost to the claimant. The Article of Agreement signed by White-Man-Runs-Him authorized Byington and Wilson, a law firm in Washington,

D.C., to represent him in his claim. He authorized the form on February 27, 1922.

On April 5, 1922, the Department of Interior, Bureau of Pensions, wrote to the Adjutant General's Office, "In the above-cited claim for pension, it is alleged that White-Man-Runs-Him served." The letter went on to request that the Adjutant's Office provide more information, including full military history, personal description, place of birth, occupation at time of enlistment, and his military stations. The Adjutant contacted White-Man-Runs-Him's representatives, who responded with the answers on the proper form on April 15, 1922.

The correspondence and record-gathering was not finished. On May 4, 1922, Byington and Wilson received another letter from the Bureau of Pensions which advised them the War Department had no record of any Indian scout under the name of White-Man-Runs-Him. The letter went on to ask whether or not he had served or enlisted under any other name, and if so, what name did he use? Requests were also made for his date of enlistment and date of discharge, and finally they demanded the scout forward his discharge certificate to the bureau. White-Man-Runs-Him was not certain he had ever received a discharge form or paper. He recalled that he had been given a piece of buckskin with some writing on it which might have represented official discharge, but after carrying it with him for some time, it finally deteriorated and he threw it away.

Another eight months passed before the questions were finally answered in the best way possible. Big Medicine, a 68-year-old Crow who had known White-Man-Runs-Him all of his life, signed the first of two affidavits on White-Man-Runs-Him's behalf. The second affidavit was signed by White Woman, also 68 years old, who duplicated Big Medicine's oath which among other things included his original Crow name, White Buffalo That Turns Back.

The information required by the Bureau was received and in order. White-Man-Runs-Him was getting used to the paper work. By now, he had provided the authorities with his original declaration, a power of attorney statement, family data, report of service, two affidavits, a statement that he had no record of birth, and an explanation that his discharge papers had been lost.

Further correspondence points to the fact that the Pensions Bureau was confused, incompetent, or both. They relayed a letter to the Adjutant General requesting a "further search for the records of the Sioux named White Buffalo That Turns Back." On March 20, 1923, the commissioner wrote asking for the Indian equivalent of the name White-Man-Runs-Him. They made it a point to ask for a discharge certificate.

C. H. Asbury, Superintendent, Crow Agency, returned a letter explaining once again the discharge papers had been lost long ago, and that there would have been no way White-Man-Runs-Him could have preserved them. Having viewed the correspondence, and understanding the situation, the assistant commissioner wrote to the commissioner, "This office will be glad to be informed of your final disposition of this claim for pension."

The records indicate U.S. Senator John B. Kendrick, of Wyoming, intervened on White-Man-Runs-Him's behalf, probably at the request of White-Man-Runs-Him's law firm. Kendrick phoned the Pension Bureau. Whatever the message of this call, Kendrick received a letter two days later, on May 2, 1923, from the commissioner. The commissioner told Senator Kendrick, "Evidence filed in support of this claim is being examined and considered by the Board of Review for final settlement, and both you and the claimant will be promptly advised of the result."

But on May 9, the Chief of the Board of Review requested further investigation to determine whether the claimant was the man he said he was. The Board was still worried by the fact there were no discharge papers. They also questioned the witness Big Medicine, citing verification had been made in the field.

Special Examiner, M. M. Brower, sought out the proper Montana authorities who sent examiner William Selvey to gather a report on White-Man-Runs-Him to determine his authenticity.

On September 1, and again on September 6, 1923, Senator Kendrick wrote to Pension Commissioner Gardner and to Hays Haymaker, the Commissioner of Special Examination. Haymaker returned a letter to Kendrick telling him the examiner "did not trust Big Horn Country, Montana." He further told the Senator a "visit would be made to the home of White-Man-Runs-Him where they would secure his statement, and fully explain the requirements." Selvey first met with White-Man-Runs-Him on September 12, 1923. His conversations and investigation produced an exhaustive report which was not completed until October 18, 1923. The final deposition was signed by Tom LeForge, who had campaigned with White-Man-Runs-Him when he scouted for Gibbon, Custer, and Miles against the Sioux and Cheyenne.

Selvey gave his report to the Commissioner of Pensions on October 19, at which time he recommended "consideration" of the report. By November 7, the report was referred to the Chief of the Board of Review, M. L. Dawkins. Finally, on November 15, 1923, White-Man-Runs-Him received what was due him. After two years of paperwork and bureaucratic mistrust, he was to receive a pension of $20 per month, although he would be somewhat compensated for the delays with pay retroactive to May 31, 1920.

As the years went by, the health of White-Man-Runs-Him began to fail. The records show a claim on his behalf was made by William Fletcher and Company, Washington, D.C., for an increase in pension due to the "claimant's physical condition and age. The claim was filed on May 10, 1927. The claim filled out on May 6, stated White-Man-Runs-Him, now about 75 years of age, was wholly unable to earn support. The claim said he had a "tubercular condition partially due to an accident resulting in broken ribs, combined with old age effects and poor eyesight." Robert Yellowtail witnessed the claim.

By this time Winfield Scott was the Commissioner of Pensions. On February 17, 1928, he informed Fletcher and company he awaited the certificate of medical examination which was ordered by him on December 19, 1927, to be conducted by the Indian School Surgeon at Crow Agency, Montana.

The medical exam took place on February 29, 1928. The medical report noted that White-Man-Runs-Him had been kicked in the chest by a horse in 1921, breaking his ribs. His eyesight, according to the record, had been failing for the past eight years. While his poor eyesight had been blamed on a bug that had penetrated the eye, White-Man-Runs-Him also mentioned he had "looked through the field glasses too much." The doctor, listed in the report that in his judgement, senility had prevented him from working for the past eight to 10 years. His height was listed as 6', but his weight was not mentioned. His pulse rate was 92-100; respiration 40; blood pressure, systolic 90, diastolic 60; and his temperature was 98. His general appearance was described as feeble; nutrition poor; muscular development poor; carriage stooped; and posture stooped. Cataracts were forming in both of his eyes. His ears, nose, throat, and cardiovascular system were described as normal. Respiratory problems were noted. There was, according to the doctor, practically no expansion of the lungs, and hemorrhaging was sometimes apparent. The digestive and nervous systems seemed good and no rheumatism was apparent. The report was concluded with no evidence of venereal disease, hernias, flat feet, or varicose veins.

Because of his weakened condition, the doctor, Ira Nelson, made his examination in White-Man-Runs-Him's home. He and Pretty Medicine Pipe had moved from their country home, because of White-Man-Runs-Him's illness, to be closer to the doctor at Crow Agency. The move also benefited Pretty Medicine Pipe, whose sister could now help with any care which might be needed. Dr. Nelson noted how White-Man-Runs-Him was able to move from room to room in the house, but with difficulty. Nelson, in his final report, recommended total disability to the Pension Commission.

Scott Leavitt, Montana Chairman of the House of Representatives Committee on Indian Affairs, wrote to the Pension Bureau on March 3, 1928. Leavitt put pressure to bear on the process by asking for advice as to which act White-Man-Runs-Him should file under to receive an increase.

Leavitt was advised on March 9 that White-Man-Runs-Him was now "in receipt of $30 per month, the rate provided under the act of March 3, 1927, for those 68 years of age." Winfield Scott told Leavitt that he had not yet received a medical report from the surgeon in Crow Agency. He added that as soon as he heard from Montana, he would give the request immediate consideration. While Scott had not yet received the report on April 18, he told Leavitt the Board of Review was meeting. The apparent pressure worked. On April 28, White-Man-Runs-Him was granted a pension of $50 per month retroactive to May 10, 1927.

The process had been slow and indicative of prejudice and discrimination; however, with the help of legal council, the support of friends and relatives, and the intervention of several congressmen, White-Man-Runs-Him was successful.

SOURCES

Chapter XIV

Department of Interior Bureau of Pensions. Records contained by Bishop Henry Whipple Veterans Administration Regional office, Federal Building, Fort Snelling, St. Paul, Minnesota. File XC-2625-742.
Contains White-Man-Runs-Him's claim for pension, letters of correspondence, and medical reports.

Pension For Indian War Veterans. House of Representatives, 64th Congress, 1st session, Report No. 115, February 3, 1916.
Qualifies White-Man-Runs-Him for pension.

XV. THE CONVERSION AND DEATH

White-Man-Runs-Him had always followed the traditional Crow religious views, but exposure to the white man, his wife's conversion, and an interest in the works of the Petzoldt's in the mission field on the reservation tempered his view of Christianity and caused him to search his thoughts. He was fascinated with the white faith and respectful of its traditions and beliefs, often comparing them with his own and the values taught him as a traditional Crow.

He sometimes attended church services in Lodge Grass with his wife, Pretty Medicine Pipe. Even as he listened to the miracles of the Bible, he thought of the powers of Crow medicine in an earlier time. There was the case of "Scar Face" or "Bird Face," a teenager who fell into a campfire, causing terrible burns and later scars to his face. Youngsters made fun of Scar Face until one day he disappeared. The old people believed that he had drowned, or been killed by a bear, or perhaps even captured by an enemy.

Several years went by. Scar Face was forgotten by most. Then one day a man was seen watching the tribe from the top of Black Canyon. At first, he could not be approached. Finally he came back. It was Scar Face. He said he was coming back to the tribe, but he must do something first. He left again and went up to the Medicine Wheel in the Big Horns. Here he fasted. When he had finished, he returned to the bench below where he built a six-spoke Medicine Wheel (the Wheel is still in place and used by vision seekers and those who are in meditation). As Scar Face fasted and prayed at the Medicine Wheel he himself had built, his scars disappeared and he became a handsome young man. He returned to his tribe to live out the rest of his life.

White-Man-Runs-Him pondered other stories including the Crow, "Holy Man," who walked on water across the Little Big Horn River, in an earlier time. Was the power of the white religion any greater than that of the Crow or was it the same power open to all religions? White-

Man-Runs-Him concluded it was the same, and that there were many ways to give thanks for the sacredness of life.

Dr. W. A. Petzoldt described the church attendance of White-Man-Runs-Him as irregular. Petzoldt, minister of the Lodge Grass Baptist Church, often invited White-Man-Runs-Him to "come forward and accept Christ as his Savior." When Petzoldt called him, White-Man-Runs-Him would "appear upset, then stand up, and walk out of the Church." When Petzoldt talked to White-Man-Runs-Him one to one about personal acceptance of a Savior, he "would make no reply."

In 1926, White-Man-Runs-Him became seriously ill. The doctors were well aware he had serious complications as described earlier and might not survive. Missionaries visited him during this time and constantly reminded him of his need for a Savior. Finally, when asked if he would like them to pray for him, he nodded his approval. As missionaries kneeled to pray, they noticed White-Man-Runs-Him had raised his right hand. When the prayers were finished and the missionaries stood up, the hand was still raised. White-Man-Runs-Him asked if he might say a few words. Then pointing to Pretty Medicine Pipe, who was beside him, he said, "For many years I let her walk the Jesus road alone. That is not good. Today I, too, give myself to God, and as long as He lets me live, I walk in the Jesus road with her." His granddaughter, Winona Plenty Hoops, "told him that she was going to be baptized and join the church. White-Man-Runs-Him replied he loved her, and it was not right she should be baptized alone. He, White-Man-Runs-Him, would go with her when the time came."

Relatives and friends began to gather, as was custom, fearing that the end was near. One day, as his wife and two others sat with him he said, "I know why you are sitting here; you are waiting for me to die. You can go home now because I am not going to die for three more years." White-Man-Runs-Him slowly improved, and when his strength permitted, began to attend services. He made public confession of his faith in Christ, and the following summer was baptized in the waters of the Little Big Horn, the same river which years earlier flowed with the blood of the Seventh Cavalry. His son, John-Spies-On-The-Enemy-Strong, and his granddaughter, Winona Plenty Hoops, were baptized with him. John requested at his baptism he might become a missionary, dedicating his life to the older Crow people who were on the "sunset" trail.

In 1927, a new baptist mission was erected. Perhaps considering the failure of the Wanamaker Memorial, White-Man-Runs-Him wished to have something in the mission as a memorial to himself. It was suggested to him he should save his money for the stained glass window in the belfry tower. When the time came, he managed to save $7 of the $125 cost of the window. Government service people and friends gladly made up the difference. The window, which was lighted from the inside of the tower, could be viewed by trains passing through Lodge Grass on the Burlington Railway. The window had a large tepee in the foreground with an Indian village in the background and a cross in the sky. The window was designed by White-Man-Runs-Him. He said if anyone should ask about the window and cross that they should be told, "White-Man-Runs-Him wanted it just

Lodge Grass Baptist Church where White-Man-Runs-Him attended services. His window can be seen below the steeple.

A photograph of the glass window in the Lodge Grass Baptist Church. White-Man-Runs-Him used a variety of colors to create this beautiful scene.

where it is to tell all of us it is only the man who died on the cross that can save the people who live in the tepee."

When the church [Chivers Memorial Chapel] was dedicated in 1928, White-Man-Runs-Him was one of the main speakers. During the three-day celebration, he presented Governor J. E. Erickson with a beautiful shirt.

In an impressive ceremony, he presented Dr. W. A. Petzoldt with a beautiful bonnet. As he presented the bonnet, he also gave Dr. Petzoldt his name. According to Rev. John Frost (Plenty Crows), a Crow Baptist missionary at Pryor:

> The greatest honor an Indian Chief can confer upon a white man, an honor higher than any mere gift of a war bonnet or other token, is to give him his Indian name. When he thus gives away his name he can never use it himself again but must take another by which he will be known from that time on. This is in accordance with

tribal custom and tradition, but the instances where Indians have so singularly honored white men have been very rare.

In presenting the name, White-Man-Runs-Him said:

> My friend, after knowing you for 25 years and watching your life and your work among my people, I feel the time has come to give you my name. You have won my heart, not so much by what you have said but by the pure and unselfish lives you and your good wife have lived among us Crows. When a Chief gives away his name he chooses a man with a high rank and a good, clean record. I feel that you fill all these requirements. I now name you White-Man-Runs-Him, a name which I have guarded so it would be respected by my tribesmen and all that knew me. My heart is full of joy to know that I am leaving my name with a man as worthy of it as you are.

White-Man-Runs-Him now publicly took the name given by his people to Crook and to Custer — Morning Star. Until his death he would be called Morning Star.

Dr. Petzoldt often said he became one of the strongest Christians of the tribe. "No unsaved Indian ever came to his home without being urged to accept Christ as Savior."

On May 1, 1929, the commissioner of Indian Affairs in a letter to Edward Moyan, Acting Commissioner of Pensions said he received a note from the superintendent of the Crow Agency, telling him White-Man-Runs-Him was quite feeble and there was doubt as to how long he might live. The letter pleaded White-Man-Runs-Him's request to be buried in the Custer Battlefield National Cemetery. The letter mentioned:

> It seems the custodian is not allowed to accept a body for burial there without a discharge paper as evidence. If his discharge, or copy thereof, or a certificate in lieu of last discharge is filed with his pension claim, this office would like to have you furnish us a copy of same for Indian Scout. If not on file, please advise what your records show as to the date, etc., of his discharge, the dates of service and the names under which he was enlisted and discharged.

Moyan returned a letter on May 7 that no discharge certificate had been filed. The appropriate information from War Department records was, however, given.

White-Man-Runs-Him shown wearing two of the three coats made for him by his wife Pretty Medicine Pipe. His home is shown in the background of the top picture. (Photos courtesy of the Archives of the Board of National Ministries, American Baptist Historical Society.)

Winona Plenty Hoops remembered the day when several men came from Washington on the train to meet White-Man-Runs-Him in Lodge Grass. White-Man-Runs-Him and a number of other scouts went to the Custer Battlefield to pick their grave sites. Many were superstitious and refused to select their sites, but White-Man-Runs-Him picked his spot right away. He declared he wanted to be buried under the flag he loved, so it might, for all time, fly over his grave.

The way had been paved for the old scout to be buried with the other Crow scouts of the Seventh Cavalry at the Custer Battlefield National Monument. With a number of relatives in attendance at his bedside, White-Man-Runs-Him died on June 2, 1929. He had predicted several years earlier that he would live three more years. He died several months short of his prediction.

White-Man-Runs-Him had been a warrior. Throughout his youth and for some time during his adult years, White-Man-Runs-Him had expected to be buried in the traditional way. He would be dressed in his finest clothes and painted. If he died in his lodge, his body would be wrapped in his tepee cover and he would be taken out under the side of the tepee. The old ways taught that to go out the entrance would bring death to some person in the same lodge. If he had died as a warrior on the field of battle, he would be laid outside and painted there, holding a feathered fan. In this case the entire camp would mourn his death.

His relatives in mourning would cut their hair and often chop off a finger-joint. They sometimes gashed their legs, arms, and foreheads. In the old days, the relatives would leave the camp for several months to continue their mourning, which often lasted a year or more. When they returned, the relatives would distribute their possessions to the tribe, retaining only their clothing and medicine.

After his body had been dressed, it would be placed on a scaffold or four forked poles. It might also have been placed in the fork of a tree. The head would face the west with the feet pointing to the east. After decomposition of the corpse, the bones were often gathered and placed in protective rock barricades or in caves. There were many cases in which the retrieved bones were simply buried in the earth. But for White-Man-Runs-Him and the Crow, these were no longer traditional times. White-Man-Runs-Him had adapted to the changes that occurred around him. He would not be buried in the old way.

His wish to be buried with full military honors was realized on June 4, with White-Man-Runs-Him American Legion Post 116, Lodge Grass, providing full military honors. The post had been named White-Man-Runs-Him years earlier as an honor to the well-known scout. The Legion was not created until 1917 and originally included veterans who were in service from April 6, 1917 to November 11, 1918. Scouts of the Indian Wars were not eligible for membership. White-Man-Runs-Him had, however, a real affection for the post and on occasions attended meetings.

Dr. William Petzoldt, his old friend, officiated at the funeral attended by family members and many other dignitaries. He was buried near the flag, in lot 1467, the place he had selected. Newspapers throughout the nation carried the story of the old scout passing on to the spirit world and his service to the U.S. flag. People consoled each other and many noteworthy people wrote to each other bemoaning the loss of this popular and respected scout.

As soon as White-Man-Runs-Him died, Superintendent C. H. Asbury wrote the Bureau of Pensions returning White-Man-Runs-Him's pension check. With the death of White-Man-Runs-Him, Pretty Medicine Pipe discovered she would have to go through almost the same process to gain a pension that her husband had gone through.

The declaration was taken by Asbury, at the Crow Agency, on June 27, 1929. On September 24, 1929, E. W. Young, Field Representative, Special Examination Division, received a letter from the Chief of Special Examinations. The letter raised the question of the identity of Pretty Medicine Pipe as the legal claimant and widow of the scout. On November 5, 1929, C. H. Asbury wrote the commissioner inquiring as to the claim of Pretty Medicine Pipe.

The Commissioners emphasized she was old and bothered by rheumatism, the winter was coming on, and that she would like her claim approved. Asbury received a letter from Earl Church, Commissioner, on November 15 that a special examination to determine the merits of the case would have to take place.

Again, Senator Leavitt became involved. In a letter dated January 21, he strongly requested information on the pension status, noting the papers had been forwarded from Montana in June, 1929. On January 24, Leavitt heard from Commissioner Church that the claim was being examined.

Senator Wheeler, Montana, also wrote an urgent letter to Church on April 4, 1930, saying, "Will you kindly give this claim your attention and if possible, have action taken thereon expedited?" He enclosed a letter from John Carpenter, Lodge Grass, for the commissioner's information. On April 8, 1930, Senator Wheeler received his answer. In short, it said that the field representative was pretty busy in North Dakota and Montana, and the special examination will be taken up as soon as possible.

On April 14, 1930, Senator Walsh of Montana wrote to Church enclosing a letter from Simon Old Crow urging a quick response. He received a letter stating that Pretty Medicine Pipe would be called upon soon. On the 16th of July, 1930, field representative Pendleton finally called upon Pretty Medicine Pipe, had her fill out a form, and recommended her consideration. Enclosed in her deposition was the will of White-Man-Runs-Him.

Pretty Medicine Pipe was thereby pensioned at $30 per month retroactive to the death of White-Man-Runs-Him. The records show she died on April 2, 1943. Since there was no record in the division of any other beneficiary, the payee was dropped from the pension roles.

Pretty Medicine Pipe had been a medicine woman among the Crow. She not only doctored people, but also played an instrumental role in a number of ceremonies. Prior to her death, she passed her powers and responsibilities along to Winona Plenty Hoops.

With the death of Pretty Medicine Pipe, many of White-Man-Runs-Him's personal possessions including his medicine bundle, headdress, and several coats made of elk and beaver fur by Pretty Medicine Pipe were packed in three trunks and stored in Winona's father's shed. Two of the trunks were later moved to another relative's residence where they were stolen. It is believed White-Man-Runs-Him's possessions made their way to the pawn shops of Billings or other such communities before ending up in the hands of collectors who probably had no idea what they had obtained. Many of

6-1142

File allot.
#1602

@ $50 to 7/4/29

Crow Agency, Montana,
June 8, 1929.

Bureau of Pensions,
Office of Disbursing Clerk,
Washington, D. C.

Sir:

I am returning herewith pension check #18,141,194, in favor of Whiteman Runs Him, #11785.

This is to report that Whiteman Runs Him died June 2, about 5:30 or 6 P.M. While this pension check is doubtless for the month of May, we felt we should take no chances on endorsing it for him, though ordinarily with our own Department checks we would have endorsed it as Superintendent, he being a trust Indian of this Tribe.

His wife is Pretty Medicine Pipe and I trust you can re-issue this check in her favor or to myself as Superintendant for his account and it will be handled on the books for payment to the heirs or applied in the payment of some funeral expenses which have not been met, however your regulations permit.

I have no doubt his wife, Pretty Medicine Pipe, will call upon us in a very short time, wanting to apply for a pension as his widow. There will be no difficulty in establishing the fact that she was his widow, regularly married to him, and was living with him as his wife at the time of his death, and if it is probable she would be entitled to a widow's pension, we had as well put the matter in motion now as later and if you will have the proper papers sent to me, I will prepare them promptly.

Very respectfully,

Superintendent.

CHA:FM
Encl.

210

~~DEPOSITION OF~~   Certificate of Search   , ~~CONTINUATION SHEET~~

As legal widowhood is an issue in this case, I am presenting the last will

and testament of White Man Runs Him as evidence in the case.

I, White Man Runs Him of the Crow Agency State of Montana, being of sound
mind, relizing the uncertainties of human life, do make this my last Will and
Testament, hereby revoking all former wills by me made, in manner and form
following, that is to say:
First I desire that all my legal depts bepaid, including the expences of
my last illness, funeral and burial.
Second I give, devise, and bequeath to my wife PRETTY MEDICINE PIPE the
following described real estate, where my home is of my allotment # 1602.
Lot 4 and SW$\frac{1}{4}$ of SE$\frac{1}{4}$ of section 10. Twp. 7 S, Range 35. (306.53 acres .)
Lot 1 and 2 and NW$\frac{1}{4}$ of NE$\frac{1}{4}$ of Sec. 15, Twp 7 S, Range 35, and
my 1/5 interest of Bull Chief allotment No. 1784.
I give, devise, and bequeath all of the rest and residue of my estate, real,
personal, and mixed, to John Whitman, son, Tillie Whitman Pease, daughter. and
Margaret Spotted Horse, Step daughter, each an undivided 1/3 interest in the
following land:
Lot 1, 2, 3, and 4, and E$\frac{1}{2}$ and E$\frac{1}{2}$ of W$\frac{1}{2}$ of Sec 31. Twp., 7S, Range 36 East
containing 621.96 acres.
All personal property to go to my wife PRETTY MEDICINE PIPE.

In witness wherof I WHITE MAN RUNS HIM, have hereunto set my hand, sealed,
published, and declared this to be my Last Will and Testament This 11th day of
January 1927

                                              His
                        White Man Runs Him
                                              Mark

I certify that this is a true and correct copy of the Will of White Man Runs Him

Crow Agency Montana   *Charles A. Pendleton*
July 21, 1930   Field Representative.

Census Records of Crow Indians for the year 1886 show PRETTY MEDICINE PIPE
as being 28 at that time.

                        Charles A. Pendleton
                        Field Representative

MLB

DEPARTMENT OF THE INTERIOR
BUREAU OF PENSIONS

Indian Widow Original No. 1647276, Pretty-Medicine Pipe

    Crow Indian Agency, Crow Agency, Big Horn County, Montana

                           Northen Cheyennes & Sioux Campaign

as widow of White-Man-Runs-Him (Mahr-stah-shee-dah-ku-roosh) Pvt., Indian Scts.USA

In cases submitted for special examination the papers should be indexed to show page numbers, names and addresses of claimants and witnesses, dates of filing, and subjects covered, a separate index being required for each brief. In indexing surgeons' certificates, dates of examination, not of filing, should be stated.

---

1. Widow's Declaration, Act of March 3, 1927, July 23, 1929, claimant alleges: That she is 71 yrs. old; born during 1858, on the Missouri River in the musselshell country, no town near them; wid. of White-Man-Runs-Him (Mahr-stah-shee-dah-ku-roosh) who enl. Apr. 10, 1876 at Crow Agency, Mont. Ty. under that name with Gen. Geo. A. Custar; dis. Sept. 30, 1876, after campaign against the Sioux and Cheyenne Indian of Mont.; died June 2, 1929 at his home near Lodge Grass, Mont.; mar. to sol. about 18 yrs. ago by Rev. Burgess, under name of Pretty Medicine Pipe at Crow Agency, Mont.; White Man Runs Him was mar, before but he divorced her and later mar. Pretty Medicine Pipe. Clmt's first husband died before she mar. White Man Runs Him; no children; no World War service for self or fam.

2. C. H. Asbury, Supt., Crow Indian Agency, Crow Agency, Mont. , July 23, 1929, transmitting above declaration with information he is unable to give exact dates of claimant's marriage to White Man Runs Him about 18 yrs. ago.

3. Marriage circular dated Apr. 15, 1922 of White Man Runs Him, gives birth at Edgar, Mont. in spring of 1855; enl. in Co. X, V Reg. U. S. Inf., Scout, U. S. A. married to Pretty Medicine Pipe Oct. 15, 1904 at Crow Agency, Mont., by Mr. Burgess, where records may be found; previously married to Horse by Indian custom, from whom he was divorced, not on record; present wife previousley mar. to Spotted Horse by Indian custom, dates not on record; died 1902; children as follows:

        Mrs. Tillie Pease, born 1888, living
        John White Man Runs Him, born 1893, living
        Blake White Man Runs Him, born 1892, living.

White-Man-Runs-Him's pictures that he had collected from his many trips as a delegate to Washington, his participation in parades, celebrations, and dedications were destroyed when one of his homes burned some time ago. Fortunately, relatives still possess some duplicates. His prized peace medal, his knife, and whip are still in the hands of relatives, as are two of the tepees he owned. The tepees are now in the process of being refurbished.

The legacy of White-Man-Runs-Him is alive and well in the land of the Crow. Joe Medicine Crow notes that requests for him to speak about the Crow scouts who led Custer have recently increased. He has told the stories at the Little Big Horn and other locations throughout the country.

White-Man-Runs-Him still has five living grandchildren. Together with their children and grandchildren, they meet several times a year to celebrate and discuss the life of White-Man-Runs-Him. Even now they are searching for the descendents of White-Man-Runs-Him's wives to bring the families together so they might better understand his life and its meaning for them. As has been discussed previously, White-Man-Runs-Him was not close to his own family. When a divorce took place in traditional times, such closeness with former family members often did not continue. White-Man-Runs-Him developed a closer relationship with Pretty Medicine Pipe's family than with his own. Today, this may be hard to understand, but now his descendents continue to try to rebuild these family ties.

The relatives of White-Man-Runs-Him have increased status today because they are the descendants of a noted warrior. When they gather, they still sing his honor song. In earlier times special singers and drummers made up songs to honor and extol the virtues, accomplishments, and war deeds of a warrior. When an important event took place or a celebration was held, the song would be sung. The honored warrior would get up and dance as the singers repeated the verses. He would often tell a good luck story and wish all who attended good luck. Sometimes the honored man would present gifts to clan uncles or special guests. When the warrior died, the relatives would continue to have the right to use the honoring song. The honoring song of White-Man-Runs-Him still is used by his gathering relatives as they come to know each other and better appreciate him.

Recently a young star basketball player used the song at a celebration for his outstanding basketball team. The song had been given to White-Man-Runs-Him shortly after the Custer fight. The song proclaims: "White-Man-Runs-Him, you scouted against the enemy, the Sioux once. Now you have scouted again."

Several years ago a man from near Hardin, Montana, was shooting pictures in the vicinity of the Crow's Nest, where White-Man-Runs-Him first sighted the Sioux and Cheyenne camp on the Little Big Horn. As the man looked toward the Crow's Nest, he saw four Indians on horseback. He was startled for a minute. Then gaining his composure, he raised his camera and took a picture. When the photo was developed, the ghostly shapes revealed the faces of White-Man-Runs-Him, Hairy Moccasin, Goes Ahead, and Curley. White-Man-Runs-Him and those who scouted with him live forever in the land of the Crow.

Joe Medicine Crow is pictured at what remains of White-Man-Runs-Him's home in the valley of the Chiefs.

Located near the flag he loved, the marker of White-Man-Runs-Him.

The burial spot of Pretty Medicine Pipe in the National Battlefield Cemetery, Little Big Horn.

SOURCES

Chapter XV

Department of Interior Bureau of Pensions. Records contained by Bishop Henry Whipple Veterans Administration Regional Office, Federal Building, Fort Snelling, St. Paul, Minnesota. File XC-2625-742.
Correspondence regarding White-Man-Runs-Him and Pretty Medicine Pipe, will of White-Man-Runs-Him, and Pretty Medicine Pipe's declaration.

Lowie, Robert. "Social Life of the Crow Indians." *Anthropological Papers American Museum of Natural History*, Vol. IX.
Contains information on traditional Crow burials.

Medicine Crow, Joseph. Personal Interview.
15 June 1991.
Stories of Scar Face, Crow who walked on water, honor song, and Crow scouts appearing on the Crow's Nest.

Petzoldt, Rev. W. A. "The Life of White-Man-Runs-Him." Funeral address prepared for the funeral of White-Man-Runs-Him by Petzoldt. The speech provided by Robert Lix, Post Adjutant, White-Man-Runs-Him Post No. 16. Lodge, Grass, Montana.
Contains information about the life of White-Man-Runs-Him and his religious faith.

Plenty Crows. "Story Of Ceremony At Which Famous Indian Scout Honored Baptist Missionary," *Billings Gazette*, May 30, 1937.

Plenty Hoops, Winona. Personal Interview.
13 June 1991.
Received information on his desire for burial, and whereabouts of his possessions.

The Department of Missionary Education (ed.). *The Moccasin Trail.* Philadelphia: The Judson Press, 1932.
Contains the story of White-Man-Runs-Him's conversion.

The Saginaw Daily News, June 4, 1929. Associated Press release on the death of White-Man-Runs-Him.

The Sheridan Post Enterprise, June 3, 1929.
Reports the death of White-Man-Runs-Him and surveys his life.

BIBLIOGRAPHY

Anderson, Gary Clayton. *Little Crow, Spokesman For the Sioux.* St. Paul: Historical Society Press, 1986.

Anderson, Gary Clayton and Alan R. Woolworth (ed.) *Through Dakota Eyes.* St. Paul: Minnesota Historical Society Press, 1988.

Appel, Joseph H. *The Business Biography of John Wanamaker Founder and Builder.* New York: The Macmillan Company, 1930.

Badhorse, Beverly. "It is Said That the Chiefs Saw Visions Of the Battle at Foreboding Medicine Rock": *Billings Gazette,* June 23, 1976.

Baker, Sue Taylor. "Battle of the Little Big Horn." *Listen* May, 1977.

Barstow, L. T. (ed.) *Journal of Fransois Antoine Laroque: From Assiniboine to the Yellowstone.* 1805. Ottawa: Government Printing Bureau, 1910.

Benjamin, Dr. John and W. W. Pendergast. "Little Crow, The Sioux Chief." *St. Paul Pioneer Press,* July 10, 1863.

Bradley, Lieut. James H. *Montana Column.* Norman: University of Oklahoma, 1962. Edited by Edgar I. Stewart.

Billings Gazette, May 27, 1961.

Billings Gazette, "Family Weekly," June 23, 1985.

"Bureau of Indian Affairs Records." Crow Agency Montana.

Buckingham, Cindy, Jan Green and Geneva Stewart. *A History Of The Crow Indians Based on Written Sources.* Lodge Grass, Montana: Lodge Grass Schools, 1972.

Catlin, George. *North American Indian.* Vol.1. New York: Dover University Inc., 1973.

Carley, Kenneth. *Little Crow, Spokesman For the Sioux.* St. Paul: The Minnesota Historical Society Press, 1976.

"Crow Agency allotment records." National Archives-Pacific North-West Region.

Curtis, Edward S. *The North American Indian.* Vol. III. New York: Johnson Reprint Corporation, 1908.

Dellit, Ursula S. *Notes from Chief Crazy Horse and Max Big Man,* June 20, 1935.

Dellitt, Ursula S. *Story of the Custer Fight.* Contains the story of the Custer fight as told to Dellitt by Ben Pease, March 16, 1934.

Department of Interior Bureau of Pensions. Records contained by Bishop Henry Whipple Veterans Administration Regional Office, Federal Building, Fort Snelling, St. Paul, Minnesota. File XC-2625-742.

Dippie, Brian W. "The Thrillin'est Fight Ever." *Annuals of Wyoming,* Vol. 54, Nov. 2, 1982.

Dixon, Joseph K. *The Vanishing Race.* New York: Popular Library, 1923.

DuBois, Charles. *Custer Mystery.* El Segundo, Cal.: Upton and Son, 1986.

Dustin, Fred. *The Custer Tragedy*. Ann Arbor. Edwards Brothers, Inc., 1939.

Ewers, John (ed.) *Five Tribes of the Upper Mississippi*. Norman: University of Oklahoma, 1961,

Fraser, Willard E. "A Squaw Did Custer In?" *Billings Gazette*, August 22, 1969.

Folwell, William Watts. *A History of Minnesota.* Vol. II. St. Paul, Minnesota. Minnesota Historical Society Press, 1924.

Graham, W. A. *The Custer Myth*. Lincoln and London: University of Nebraska Press, 1953.

Gray, John S. *Centennial Campaign*. Fort Collins: The Old Army Press. 1976.

Hanner, Kenneth. *Men With Custer*. Old Army Press, 1972.

Hardin Tribune-Herald. Hardin, Montana, August 14, 1958.

Heidenreich, Conrad. "A History of the Crow of Montana." Unpublished thesis. University of Oregon, 1974.

Hoxie, Frederick E. "Building A Future On The Past: Crow Indian Leadership in an Era of Division and Reunion." National Anthropological Archives, Bureau of Ethnology Collection.

Hyde, George. *Red Cloud's Folk*. Norman: University of Oklahoma Press, 1967.

Ketcham, Barbara. "New Finds Shed Light on Custer's Last Stand." *Star-Tribune.* Casper, Wyoming, March 30, 1975.

Keune, Manfred E. "An Immodest Proposal: A Memorial to the North American Indian." A paper presented to the Popular Culture Association, Annual Convention, Baltimore, 1977.

"Last of Great Indian Chiefs to Gather for Memorial." February 21, 1918. Unknown article, National Battlefield, Lodge Grass, Montana.

Lawson, Publius V. "The Winnebago Tribe." *Wisconsin Archaeologist.* Vol. 4, No. 3. Milwaukee: Wisconsin Archaeological Society, 1907.

LeForge, Thomas. *Memoirs of a White Crow Indian*. Lincoln and London: University of Nebraska, 1974.

Letter received from Richard A. Beulke, Al Bedoo Temple, Ancient Order Nobles of Mystic Shrine, Billings, Montana. October 14, 1991.

Letter written by Robert Bruce, author, to General Godfrey. August 15, 1928. In files of National Battlefield, Crow Agency, Montana.

Libby, O. G. *The Arikara Narrative Of The Campaign Against The Hostile Dakotas.* June, 1876. Bismark: North Dakota Historical Collections.

Linderman, Frank B. *Plenty Coups*. Lincoln and London: University of Nebraska Press, 1930.

Linderman, Frank B. *Pretty Shield*. Lincoln and London: University of Nebraska., 1932.

Lowie, Robert. "The Religion of the Crow." *Anthropological Paper American Museum of Natural History*. Vol. XXV. 1922.

Lowie, Robert. "Social Life of the Crow Indians." *Anthropological Paper American Museum of Natural History.* Vol. IX.

Lowie, Robert. "Societies of the Crow Hidatsa and Mandan Indians." *Anthropological Paper American Museum of Natural History.* Vol. XI.

Lowie, Robert. *The Crow Indians.* Lincoln and London: University of Nebraska Press, 1935.

Marquis, Arnold. *A Guide to American Indians.* Norman: University of Oklahoma Press, 1978.

Marquis, Thomas B. *Keep The Last Bullet For Yourself.* Algonac, Michigan: Reference Publications, Inc., 1976.

Mc Allester, David. "Water as a Disciplinary Agent among the Crow and Blackfoot." *American Anthropologist.* N.S. 43, 1941.

Medicine Crow, Joseph. Interview with Crow Elder. 31 August 1965.

Medicine Crow, Joseph. Letter. 6 September 1991.

Medicine Crow, Joseph. *Medicine Crow.* Lodge Grass, Montana: Crow Central EducationCommission, 1979.

Medicine Crow, Joseph. Personal Interview. June 1987 – June 1991.

Medicine Crow, Joseph. Personal Interviews. June 1989 and 17 June 1990.

Medicine Crow, Joseph. Personal Interviews. 16 June 1990 and 19 June 1991.

Medicine Crow, Joseph. Personal Interview. 18 June 1990.

Medicine Crow, Joseph. Personal Interview. 14 June 1991.

Medicine Crow, Joseph. Personal Interview. 15 June 1991.

Medicine Crow, Joseph. Personal Interviews. 16 – 17 June 1991.

Medicine Crow, Joseph. Personal Interview. 17 June 1991.

Medicine Crow, Joseph. "Statement of John B. Cummings." Mimeographed: June 25, 1983.

Medicine Crow, Joseph. "The Crow Migration Story." Big Woods/Big Plains lecture series. Stillwater, Minnesota. 9 April 1988.

Medicine Crow, Joseph. "White-Man-Runs-Him." Big Woods/Big Plains lecture series. Stillwater, Minnesota. 10 April 1990.

Meyer, Roy. *History of the Santee Sioux.* Lincoln: University ofNebraska, 1967.

Miller, David Humphreys. *Custer's Fall.* Lincoln and London: University of Nebraska, 1957.

Nabokov, Peter. *Two Leggings.* Lincoln and London: University of Nebraska Press, 1967.

New York Herald. June 6, 1909.

New York Times. February 23, 1913.

New York Tribune. May 29, 1909.

Pension For Indian War Veterans. House of Representatives, 64th Congress, 1st session. Report No. 115, February 3, 1916.

Petzoldt, Rev. W. A. "The Life of White-Man-Runs-Him." Funeral address prepared for the funeral of White-Man-Runs-Him by Petzoldt.

Philadelphia North American. May 14, 1909.

Plenty Crows. "Story Of Ceremony at Which Famous Indian Scout Honored Baptist Missionary." *Billings Gazette.* May 30, 1937.

Plenty Hoops, Winona. Personal Interview. 13 June 1991.

Radin, Paul. "The Winnebago Tribe." *Bureau of American Ethnology, 37th Annual Report.* 1915 – 16. Washington: Government Printing Office, 1923.

Reynolds, Charles R. Jr. *American Indian Portraits From The Wanamaker Expedition of 1913.* Brattleboro, Vermont: The Stephen Green Press, 1971.

Richards, Raymond. "Picturesque Celebration of Red Men's Last Triumph in the West Is Given Where Custer Offered Full Measure." *Billings Journal.* June 26, 1916.

Robinson, Doane. *A History of the Dakota or Sioux Indians.* Minneapolis: Reprint, Ross and Haines, 1967.

Sandoz, Mari. *Cheyenne Autumn.* New York: Hastings House, 1953.

Schoenberger, Dale. "Custer's Scouts." *Montana the Magazine ofWestern History.* Spring, 1966.

Sneve, Virginia Driving Hawk. *They Led A Nation.* Sioux Falls: Brevet Press, Inc., 1975.

Stewart, Edgar I. *Custer's Luck.* Norman: University of Oklahoma Press, 1957.

Superintendent's Annual Narrative and Statistical Reports. Records Group 75, National Archives.

"The Crow." *Sheridan Post.* 10 July 1902.

The Department of Missionary Education (ed.) *The Moccasin Trail.* Philadelphia: The Judson Press, 1932.

The Saginaw Daily News. June 4, 1929.

The Sheridan Post Enterprise. June 3, 1929.

The Tepee Book. *Fiftieth Anniversary of the Custer Battle.* Vol. 11. No. VI., June, 1916.

Upton, Richard (ed.) *The Indian as a Soldier at Fort Custer* Montana, 1890-95. Elsegundo, Cal.: Upton and Sons, 1983.

Vestal, Stanley. *Sitting Bull.* Norman and London: University of Oklahoma Press, 1957.

Willert, James. *Little Big Horn Diary.*Whittier: Spectrum Silk Screen, 1977.

Wissler, Clark. *Indians of the United States.*Garden City: Doubleday and Company, 1940, revised 1966.

Wanamaker, Rodman. *A Tribute to the North American Indian.* Neww York: The Royeroft Press, 1909.

TABLE OF ILLUSTRATIONS

INDEX

(Boldface entries indicate illustrations)

Wolf Lays Down, Ed, 164
Wood, Leonard, 151
Wooden Leg, 112, 156
Woodruff, C. A., 180
Woods, General, 150
Wowinape, 67
Wyola, Montana, 54, 55
Wyoming territory, 68–69

Y
Yanktons, 62
Yarlott, Charles, 164
Yellow Hair, 101

Yellow Medicine Tributary, 62
Yellowstone expedition, 70–71
Yellowstone River, 16, 19, 68, 73,
    84, 87, 120, 128, 130, 140
Yellow Swallow, 101
Yellowtail, Amy, 145
Yellowtail, Robert *(son-in-law)*,
    111, 143, 197
    as member of Crow delegation,
    157, 166–78
Young, E. W., 208
Young White Buffalo, 19